Department of the Air Force Officer Talent Management Reforms

Implications for Career Field Health and Demographic Diversity

MATTHEW WALSH, DAVID SCHULKER, NELSON LIM, ALBERT A. ROBBERT, RAYMOND E. CONLEY, JOHN S. CROWN, CHRISTOPHER E. MAERZLUFT

Prepared for the Department of the Air Force
Approved for public release; distribution unlimited

 PROJECT AIR FORCE

For more information on this publication, visit **www.rand.org/t/RRA556-1**.

About RAND

The RAND Corporation is a research organization that develops solutions to public policy challenges to help make communities throughout the world safer and more secure, healthier and more prosperous. RAND is nonprofit, nonpartisan, and committed to the public interest. To learn more about RAND, visit www.rand.org.

Research Integrity

Our mission to help improve policy and decisionmaking through research and analysis is enabled through our core values of quality and objectivity and our unwavering commitment to the highest level of integrity and ethical behavior. To help ensure our research and analysis are rigorous, objective, and nonpartisan, we subject our research publications to a robust and exacting quality-assurance process; avoid both the appearance and reality of financial and other conflicts of interest through staff training, project screening, and a policy of mandatory disclosure; and pursue transparency in our research engagements through our commitment to the open publication of our research findings and recommendations, disclosure of the source of funding of published research, and policies to ensure intellectual independence. For more information, visit www.rand.org/about/principles.

RAND's publications do not necessarily reflect the opinions of its research clients and sponsors.

Preface

The Air Force is implementing extensive changes to the way it manages officer development and promotion.[1] These changes include splitting the Line of the Air Force into six separate developmental categories and applying new personnel management flexibilities as introduced by the John S. McCain National Defense Authorization Act for Fiscal Year 2019. The purpose of these reforms is to allow for more flexible and suitable developmental pathways within career fields and throughout an individual officer's career.

The Air Force asked RAND Project AIR FORCE to examine the potential utility of changes to officer development and promotion management and the implications they may have for career field health and demographic diversity. Through an analysis of historical data and simulations using a novel inventory modeling tool—the Air Force Personnel Policy Simulation Tool (PPST)—RAND determined that most of these changes have the potential to benefit many career fields and demographic groups. Yet these changes may also have unanticipated effects; as a result, their implementation must be carefully monitored to ensure that they continue to address the Air Force's goals. A strategic tool like PPST is needed to prospectively explore and continuously monitor the effects of personnel policy changes.

The research reported here was commissioned by the Director of Force Development, Deputy Chief of Staff for Manpower, Personnel, and Services and conducted within the Manpower, Personnel, and Training Program of RAND Project AIR FORCE as part of a fiscal year 2019 project, "Examining the Impact of Air Force Strategic Personnel Policy Changes on Diversity and Inclusion."

RAND Project AIR FORCE

RAND Project AIR FORCE (PAF), a division of the RAND Corporation, is the Department of the Air Force's (DAF's) federally funded research and development center for studies and analyses, supporting both the United States Air Force and the United States Space Force. PAF provides the DAF with independent analyses of policy alternatives affecting the development, employment, combat readiness, and support of current and future air, space, and cyber forces. Research is conducted in four programs: Strategy and Doctrine; Force Modernization and Employment; Manpower, Personnel, and Training; and Resource Management. The research reported here was prepared under contract FA7014-16-D-1000.

---

[1] References to the Air Force throughout this document refer to the Department of the Air Force, which includes both the Air and Space Forces.

Additional information about PAF is available on our website:
www.rand.org/paf/

This report documents work originally shared with the DAF on May 20, 2020. The draft report, issued on July 15, 2020, was reviewed by formal peer reviewers and DAF subject-matter experts.

Contents

Preface iii

Figures vii

Tables ix

Summary x

Acknowledgments xii

Abbreviations xiii

1. Introduction 1

    Current Guidelines for Managing Active-Duty Officers 2

    New Flexibilities in Officer Personnel Management 3

    Research Question: How Will These Interdependent Policy Changes Affect Outcomes of
        the Personnel System? 5

    Organization of This Report 8

2. Using the PPST Promotion Model to Simulate the Near-Term Effects of Splitting the LAF 9

    Description of the Promotion Board Model 10

    Exploring the Near-Term Effects of Splitting the LAF with the PPST Promotion Model 12

    Summary 15

3. PPST Inventory Projection Capability 16

    Inventory Projection Capability 16

    Summary 23

4. Implications of Splitting the LAF for Future Inventories 24

    Effects of Splitting the LAF Broken Out by Developmental Category 25

    Effects of Splitting the LAF Broken Out by Career Field 29

    Effects of Splitting the LAF Broken Out by Gender, Race, and Ethnicity 31

    Summary 33

5. Implications of Removing Below-the-Zone Promotions and Adopting Merit-Based
    Sequencing 35

    Potential Implications of Eliminating BPZ and Adopting Merit-Based Sequencing 35

    Inventory Model Extensions 37

    Aggregate-Level Effects of Zone and Sequencing Changes 40

    Effects of Zone and Sequencing Changes Broken Out by AFSC 42

    Effects of Zone and Sequencing Changes Broken Out by Gender, Race, and Ethnicity 43

    Summary 44

6. Implications of Widening Promotion Zones 45

    Inventory Model Extensions 45

    Floors and Ceilings Needed to Shift Promotions 47

Aggregate-Level Effects of Widening Promotion Zones...49

Effects of Widening Promotion Zones Broken Out by AFSC.......................................50

Effects of Widening Promotion Zones Broken Out by Gender, Race, and Ethnicity...............51

Summary..52

7. Discussion and Future Research...54

Future Research Directions 57

Summary..58

Appendix A. Comparison of PPST with Other Approaches 59

Appendix B. PPST Promotion Model User Interface 61

Appendix C. PPST Inventory Projection Capability User Interface 69

Appendix D. Model Validation 72

References 74

Figures

Figure S.1. O-6 Inventories After Splitting the LAF and Restoring Promotion Opportunity........xi

Figure 1.1. Concept Map of Officer Development and Promotion Management.........................6

Figure 1.2. Overview of PPST 7

Figure 2.1. Entity-Level (Top) and Cohort-Level (Bottom) Depictions of
Selection Mechanism...11

Figure 2.2. Distribution of Developmental Categories by Race, Gender, and Ethnicity 14

Figure 3.1. Percentages of Accessions by AFSC from CY 2015 to CY 2019 17

Figure 3.2. Promotability Averages by AFSC and Board...19

Figure 3.3. Promotability Averages by AFSC, Demographic Category, and Board.....................20

Figure 3.4. Model-Based Cumulative Continuation Rates by AFSC (Top Panel) and by
Promotion Timing within 11X Career Field (Bottom Panel)..22

Figure 3.5. Model-Based Cumulative Continuation Rates by Gender and Race/Ethnicity 23

Figure 4.1. Selection Rates by Developmental Category, Board, and Zone 27

Figure 4.2. O-5 and O-6 Inventories by Developmental Category 27

Figure 4.3. Percentage of Officers Reaching O-6 Ahead of Due Course by
Developmental Category 28

Figure 4.4. Cumulative Continuation Rates for Air Operations and Information Warfare
Developmental Categories...29

Figure 4.5. O-5 and O-6 Inventories by AFSC 30

Figure 4.6. Selection Rates by Demographic Group, Board, and Zone 31

Figure 4.7. O-5 and O-6 Inventories by Demographic Group 32

Figure 4.8. Percentage of Officers Reaching O-6 Ahead of Due Course by
Demographic Group...33

Figure 5.1. Effects of Eliminating Below-the-Promotion-Zone and Adopting Merit-Based
Sequencing of Promotion Lists 36

Figure 5.2. Cumulative Continuation Rates Used in Model Simulations 39

Figure 5.3. Annual Separations, Promotions, and Timing in Baseline and
NoBPZ Simulations..41

Figure 5.4. Changes in O-6 Inventory Sizes by AFSC and Simulation 43

Figure 5.5. Changes in O-6 Inventory Sizes by Demographic Category and Simulation.............44

Figure 6.1. Current and Target Selection Distributions Used in Simulation.................................46

Figure 6.2. Percentage of Promotion List and Selection Rates by Consideration........................47

Figure 6.3. Percentage of Promotion List and Selection Rates by Consideration........................48

Figure 6.4. Annual Separations, Promotions, and Promotion Timing Across
Simulated Scenarios 50

Figure 6.5. Changes in O-6 Inventory Sizes by AFSC and Simulation 51
Figure 6.6. Changes in O-6 Inventory Sizes by Demographic Category and Simulation............52
Figure B.1. PPST Opening Page 61
Figure B.2. Set Opportunity Page...62
Figure B.3. Set DevCats Page 63
Figure B.4. Comparison of Attribute Frequencies 64
Figure B.5. Adjusting Attribute Weights 65
Figure B.6. Selection Rates by AFSC and Option 66
Figure B.7. Promotion Outcomes by Demographic Group and Developmental Category 67
Figure C.1. PPST Opening Page 70
Figure C.2. Inventory Projection Capability Setup Page 70
Figure C.3. Inventory Model Results Page 71
Figure D.1. Comparison of Observed and Simulated FY 2018 Inventories by Grade
        and AFSC 73

Tables

Table 1.1. Air Force Developmental Categories 4

Table 2.1. Individual and Career Field Outcomes of Promotion Policies.........................9

Table 2.2. Promotion Opportunity by Grade and Developmental Category for Historical
and Level Simulations 13

Table 2.3. Promotion Opportunity by Grade and Demographic Category for Historical and
Level Simulations 14

Table 3.1. Promotion Board Timing and Selection Rules by Grade 18

Table 4.1. Promotion Opportunity by Grade and Developmental Category for
Restore Simulation 24

Table 4.2. Selection Rates for the Air Operations and Special Warfare and the Information
Warfare Developmental Categories...26

Table 5.1. Opportunity by Grade and Developmental Category.......................................42

Table 6.1. Adjustments to Promotability Used to Produce Target Selection Distribution...........49

Table 7.1. Summary of Simulation Studies and Key Results..54

Table A.1. Comparison of Structural Modeling Tools for Simulating Personnel
Policy Changes 59

Table D.1. Observed and Simulated Selection Rates by Zone..72

Summary

Issue

The Air Force is undertaking unparalleled reforms to the way it manages officer development and promotion. As part of these reforms, the Air Force has split the Line of the Air Force (LAF), a single developmental category (DevCat) accounting for more than 80 percent of officers and 40 career fields, into six separate DevCats, and the Air Force is applying new personnel management flexibilities introduced by the John S. McCain National Defense Authorization Act for Fiscal Year 2019. The purpose of these changes is to enable the Air Force to identify, develop, and reward talent at all stages during an officer's career.

The motivations behind these personnel policy reforms are clear. However, given the complexity of officer development and promotion management, it is difficult to fully anticipate the effects of these changes. To help decisionmakers evaluate the utility and implications of new personnel policies, the RAND study team built a strategic tool called the Air Force Personnel Policy Simulation Tool (PPST) to simulate the effects of new personnel policies on career field health and demographic diversity. A tool like PPST is needed to ensure that Air Force policy changes will further stated goals to identify potentially adverse effects of personnel policy changes on career fields and demographic groups, and if needed, to develop mitigating courses of action.

Approach

In conducting its research, the study team used quantitative approaches that included

- analyzing historical data to build statistical models of promotion and retention of individuals in different career fields and demographic categories
- developing an inventory model to simulate annual officer accessions, promotion planning, promotion selection, and separation
- conducting simulations to examine how splitting the LAF into separate DevCats, adopting merit-based sequencing of promotion lists, and adopting wider promotion windows will affect career field health and demographic diversity.

Findings

- *Effects of splitting the LAF into separate DevCats on career field inventories.* Splitting the LAF may reduce selection rates for career fields that historically received more promotions and increase selection rates for those that historically received fewer promotions. Changes in selection rates, in turn, may change inventory sizes (Figure S.1.).

Figure S.1. O-6 Inventories After Splitting the LAF and Restoring Promotion Opportunity

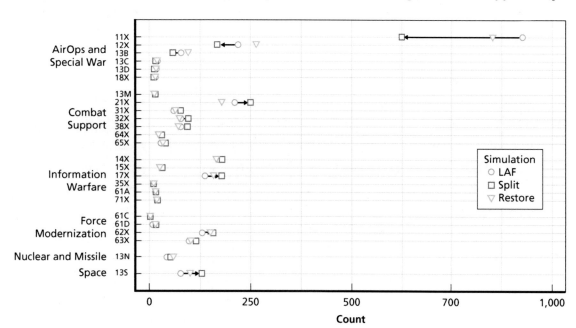

- *Effects of splitting the LAF on demographic diversity.* Because female officers and minority officers are overrepresented in career fields that have historically received fewer promotions, splitting the LAF may increase diversity at the ranks of O-5 and O-6.
- *Effects of eliminating below-the-promotion-zone (BPZ) selections and adopting merit-based sequencing on career field health.* Eliminating BPZ selections may cause officers to reach O-5 and O-6 with more years of service on average and to serve for fewer years at those grades. This in turn would mean that more annual separations would occur at O-5 and O-6 and that more promotions would be needed to maintain grade strength.
- *Effects of eliminating BPZ selections and adopting merit-based sequencing on demographic diversity.* Simulation results indicated that white female officers are expected to receive the highest percentage of BPZ selections after splitting the LAF. Consequently, the effects of replacing BPZ with merit-based sequencing may have a more negative effect for white female officers than for other demographic categories.
- *Widening promotion zones.* For officers to become competitive for promotion after first being passed, they would need to complete additional career development experiences visible to promotion boards and treated as significant growth signals.

Conclusions

- Officer management and promotion reforms may enhance the Air Force's ability to tailor developmental pathways to the needs of officers in different career fields and to identify and develop talent in officers throughout their careers.
- The implementation of these changes will affect career field health and demographic diversity in various ways, some favorably and some unfavorably.
- A strategic tool like PPST can help the Air Force to prospectively evaluate the effects of personnel policy changes.

Acknowledgments

We are grateful for the support of our sponsor, Russell Frasz, director, Force Development, Deputy Chief of Staff for Manpower, Personnel and Services, Headquarters U.S. Air Force (AF/A1D), Washington, D.C. We are also grateful for the support of Lt Gen Brian Kelly, Deputy Chief of Staff for Manpower, Personnel, and Services (AF/A1), Headquarters U.S. Air Force, Washington, D.C. Our primary contacts in AF/A1P were Brigadier General Dunn, Colonel Allee, Colonel King, and Lt Col Matthew Huibregtse. We very much appreciate their input and discussion related to this research. Our primary contacts from Force Management and Enterprise Readiness Analysis Division (A1XD) were Lt Col Jon M. Hart and Lt Col Corrie Pecoraro. We very much appreciate their help and insights as well. Finally, we thank our colleagues Tony Lawrence and Cord Thomas for their help with software development, Michael Schiefer for his help with designing the simulation model, and Kirsten Keller, John Ausink, and Miriam Matthews for their helpful comments on earlier versions of this report.

Abbreviations

AF	Air Force
AFI	Air Force Instruction
AFSC	Air Force Specialty Code
APZ	above-the-promotion-zone
BPZ	below-the-promotion-zone
CCR	cumulative continuation rates
CDE	career development experience
COA	course of action
D&I	diversity and inclusion
DevCat	developmental category
DOPMA	Defense Officer Personnel Management Act
DOR	date of rank
DRM	dynamic retention model
IPZ	in-the-promotion-zone
LAF	Line of the Air Force
MCM	Military Career Model
NDAA	National Defense Authorization Act
PPST	Personnel Policy Simulation Tool
ROPMA	Reserve Officer Personnel Management Act
TFBL	Total Force Blue-Line Model
TIG	time in grade
UI	user interface
WAPS	Weighted Airmen Promotion System
YOS	years of service

1. Introduction

The Air Force active-duty officer inventory is made up of approximately 60,000 individuals divided among more than 100 career fields.[1,2] For purposes of promotion, most career fields have historically been grouped together under a single Line of the Air Force (LAF) made up of more than 40 career fields and accounting for approximately 80 percent of officers.[3] Individuals from all career fields in the LAF were considered for promotion to field grade ranks (i.e., O-4 to O-6) at predetermined times in their careers, and they competed for a fixed number of promotions determined by the projected number of vacancies at the next highest grade.[4] The vast majority of officers selected for promotion were chosen in-the-promotion-zone (IPZ)—that is, during a one-year window determined by an officer's time in grade (TIG).[5] Thus, historically, there has been little variation in either how officers are evaluated for promotion or the timing of promotion for those selected.

The Air Force 2018 Squadron Revitalization Implementation Plan identified the importance of selecting and preparing the most talented airmen to become leaders.[6] Around the same time, Secretary of Defense James Mattis described the essential role of recruiting, developing, and retaining a high-quality workforce for warfighting success.[7] In response to these and other calls, the Air Force has begun to undertake significant talent management reform to improve its ability to identify, develop, and utilize officer talent.

In this report, we present a new tool—the Air Force Personnel Policy Simulation Tool (PPST). PPST is a personnel inventory modeling tool embedded within a user interface (UI). PPST allows users to set various promotion-related parameters and to observe the effects of those changes. The purpose of PPST is to enable Air Force analysts and decisionmakers to simulate the longitudinal effects of different policy reforms on career field health—in terms of

---

[1] Count based on the number of individuals reported in FY 2019 end-of-year personnel extracts.

[2] Air Force Personnel Center, *Air Force Officer Classification Directory (AFOCD): The Official Guide to the Air Force Officer Classification Codes*, October 31, 2018.

[3] Officers in non-LAF competitive categories (i.e., Judge Advocate General, Medical Corps, Dental Corps, Chaplains, Medical Service Corps, Biomedical Sciences Corps, and Nurse Corps) are governed by separate career management policies due to their specialized natures.

[4] U.S. Air Force, *Officer Promotions and Selective Continuation*, Air Force Instruction 36-2501, May 4, 2020.

[5] By statutory provision, no more than 10 percent of the authorized number of promotions to O-5 or O-6 may be given to officers who have not yet reached IPZ.

[6] Stephen L. Davis et al., *Improving Air Force Squadrons—Recommendations for Vitality: Report to the Chief of Staff of the United States Air Force*, 2018.

[7] Secretary of Defense James Mattis, *Summary of the 2018 National Defense Strategy of the United States of America: Sharpening the American Military's Competitive Edge*, 2018.

actual grade strength—and demographic diversity.[8] PPST combines multiple models that incorporate details from Air Force Instructions (AFIs) on officer promotion and from historical data on the developmental trajectories and retention decisions of individuals in different career fields and demographic groups. The models interact with one another to simulate the effects of changes to annual officer accession, promotion planning, selection, and separation from active duty. A tool like PPST is needed not only to ensure that Air Force policy changes will further stated goals but also to identify potentially adverse effects of personnel policy changes on career fields and demographic groups and, if needed, develop mitigating courses of action (COAs).

We briefly review current guidelines for managing active-duty officers before turning to policy changes that the Air Force has adopted or is considering adopting and that can be modeled with PPST.

Current Guidelines for Managing Active-Duty Officers

On December 12, 1980, Congress enacted the Defense Officer Personnel Management Act (DOPMA). DOPMA established uniform guidelines to govern military officer management and determine the number of field grade authorizations (O-4 through O-6) for each service. DOPMA was designed to allow services to maintain the proper mix of officers by age, grade, and experience to enable mission effectiveness and to provide career opportunities to attract and retain talented individuals.[9]

DOPMA, along with similar provisions contained in the Reserve Officer Personnel Management Act of 1994 (ROPMA), remains in effect for active-duty and reserve officers.[10] DOPMA and ROPMA have five main features.[11]

1. *Closed system.* New officers enter the inventory at low grades, and positions at higher grades are filled by internal promotion.[12]
2. *A personnel pyramid.* Grade structures for field grade officers are pyramid-shaped with fewer authorizations at higher ranks. Thus, fewer individuals are typically selected for promotion at higher ranks.[13]

---

[8] We use "demographic diversity" to refer to categories of diversity related to race, gender, and ethnicity.

[9] Bernard Rostker, Harry J. Thie, James L. Lacy, Jennifer H. Kawata, and Susanna W. Purnell, *The Defense Officer Personnel Management Act of 1980: A Retrospective Assessment.* Santa Monica, Calif.: RAND Corporation, R-4246-FMP, 1993.

[10] ROPMA was enacted in 1994 as part of the National Defense Authorization Act (NDAA) for Fiscal Year 1995 (Public Law 103-337).

[11] As summarized in Ann D. Parcell and Amanda Kraus, *Recommendations from the CNGR Implementation Plan: Exploring the Requirements of DOPMA and ROPMA*, Arlington, Va.: Center for Naval Analyses, CRM D0021641.A2, 2010.

[12] Exceptions include lateral entry above the grade of O-1 in certain professional career fields along with the flow of individuals between active-duty and reserve components.

[13] The number of individuals eligible for promotion is determined by the number in-the-promotion-zone (IPZ).

3. *A competitive, up-or-out career flow.* Officers advance through ranks by a competitive selection process. Officers twice passed over for promotion at the same grade may be forced to separate.
4. *Seniority-based promotion timing.* Officers become eligible for promotion after meeting minimum TIG requirements. Once selected, the order in which officers are promoted is determined by date of rank (DOR), with the most senior individuals being the first to pin on the new rank.
5. *Uniformity across services.* In general, DOPMA and ROPMA guidelines are applied consistently across services. This reflects the expectation that DOPMA would establish a common officer management system not tied to any one service.

DOPMA and ROPMA have indelibly shaped Air Force officer management practices and the resulting officer inventory. For example, because of the closed nature of the system, maintaining enough officers with the right knowledge and talent for senior leadership positions depends critically on the success of recruiting efforts at entry grades (and from years past). Because of the competitive nature of the system, officers with deep technical knowledge and experience who are passed over for promotion may be forced to separate. Relatedly, developmental pathways that lead to promotion may differ from developmental pathways that make an officer maximally effective in a given career field. Because of seniority-based promotion timing, officers must be promoted at predetermined points in their careers rather than when they are developmentally ready, and those not yet ready are at a disadvantage for future promotion once passed over. Finally, because of combinations of these features, career field health and demographic diversity at higher grades depend on the cumulative success of recruiting, developing and promoting, and retaining individuals from diverse backgrounds.

These limitations are not inherent in DOPMA and ROPMA. The services have developed distinct management practices within the constraints of these acts. However, as described by the Senate Armed Services Committee, the services have not taken full advantage of the flexibility that DOPMA and ROPMA offer, resulting in a closed and inflexible personnel management system.[14]

New Flexibilities in Officer Personnel Management

The John S. McCain National Defense Authorization Act (NDAA) for Fiscal Year 2019 introduced a number of new personnel policies that were intended to give services greater flexibility in how they manage officer development and promotion. These represent an attempt to overcome limitations that grew out of DOPMA and ROPMA.

As part of its effort to reform the way that officer development and promotion is managed, the Air Force is exploring applications of these flexibilities. We consider two in this report. The first is Section 504 of the FY 2019 NDAA, which allows selection boards to recommend that

---

[14] Senate Armed Services Committee, *Modernizing the Defense Officer Personnel Management Act (DOPMA)*, SASC Staff Report, undated (copy provided during a meeting of the Manpower Roundtable, November 13, 2018).

officers of particular merit be placed higher on the promotion list. This differs from the current practice of sorting promotion lists by officers' DOR and could be used to reward individuals of high merit.

The second flexibility that we consider is Section 507 of the FY 2019 NDAA, which delegates authority to service secretaries to establish alternative promotion paths for DevCats, including increasing the size of the promotion zone to allow officers to be considered multiple times for promotion. This differs from the current practice of selecting most officers for promotion during the one-year period when they are considered IPZ and could give promotion boards greater latitude to select officers for promotion when they are developmentally ready. As a separate element of its effort to reform officer development and promotion management, the Air Force has divided the 40-plus career fields making up the LAF into six separate DevCats (Table 1.1). The purpose of this change is to allow officers within different career fields to pursue tailored developmental pathways while remaining competitive for promotion.

Table 1.1. Air Force Developmental Categories

Developmental Category	Composition (Title and Career Field AFSC)
Air operations and special warfare	Pilot (11X), Combat Systems (12X), Air Battle Manager (13B), Special Tactics (13C), Combat Rescue (13D), Tactical Air Control Party (13L), Remotely Piloted Aircraft Pilot (18X)
Space operations	Space Operations (13S) and Astronaut (13A)
Nuclear and missile operations	Nuclear and Missile Operations (13N)
Information warfare	Information Operations (14F), Intelligence (14N), Weather (15W), Cyber Operations (17X), Public Affairs (35X), Operations Research Analyst (61A), Special Investigations (71S)
Combat support	Airfield Operations (13M), Aircraft Maintenance (21A), Munitions and Missile Maintenance (21M), Logistics Readiness (21R), Security Forces (31P), Civil Engineering (32E), Force Support (38F), Contracting (64P), Financial Management (65X)
Force modernization	Chemist (61C), Physicist/Nuclear Engineer (61D), Developmental Engineer (62E), Acquisition Management (63A)

SOURCE: Stephen Losey, "Farewell, Line of the Air Force: Massive Officer Category Broken Out into Six Groups," *Air Force Times*, October 21, 2019.

Research Question: How Will These Interdependent Policy Changes Affect Outcomes of the Personnel System?

To achieve policy goals, Air Force senior leaders must understand the potential downstream effects of policy changes—such as splitting the LAF and applying officer career management flexibilities allowed by the FY 2019 NDAA—throughout the Air Force career life cycle. These effects can be difficult to foresee because they often depend on the regularly recurring decisions of future managers in several organizations responsible for different aspects of the personnel system. Taken together, the purpose of PPST and this report is to help planners understand how various policy changes might unfold in a simplified version of this system, revealing the likely effects on their stated goals for career field health and demographic diversity.

Air Force Officer Management and Career Progression

PPST helps reveal policy outcomes by representing key mechanisms in the personnel system with models and by linking the models together to project how the system might holistically respond to policy changes. Figure 1.1 presents a simplified concept map of the following major mechanisms of the personnel system that affect active-duty officer development and promotion management:

- End strength is the total number of officers authorized for the Air Force at the end of the fiscal year.
- The difference between end strength and the projected officer inventory is used to determine the number of vacancies to be filled by accessions at the rank of O-1.
- After accessing, individuals enter the training pipeline to acquire technical skills needed in their career fields. Additionally, they complete career development experiences (CDEs) to prepare them for management responsibilities. The completion of training and of CDEs paired with other indicators makes individuals competitive for promotion.
- Grade strength sets the number of officers authorized for each field grade rank.
- The differences between grade strength and the projected officer population at each rank are used to determine the number of vacancies to be filled by promotions.
- Individuals twice passed over for promotion at the same grade may be forced to separate. Alternatively, individuals may choose to voluntarily separate whenever they are not constrained by an active-duty service commitment.

Figure 1.1. Concept Map of Officer Development and Promotion Management

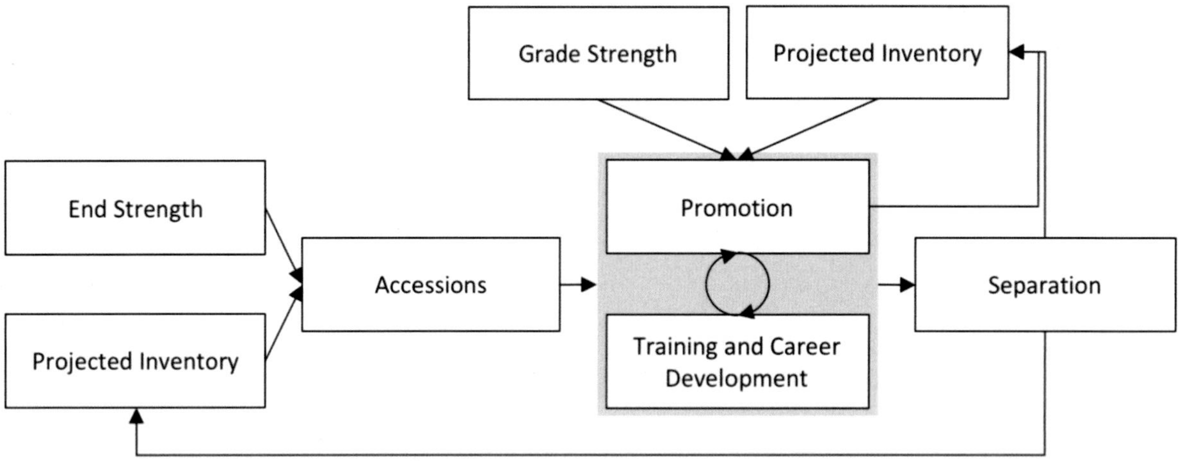

Different organizations within AF/A1, Manpower, Personnel, and Services, are concerned with different aspects of officer development and promotion management (and with different elements from the concept map in Figure 1.1).[15] Some examples are given here.

- The Directorate of Manpower, Organization, and Resources (AF/A1M) defines Air Force manpower requirements.
- The Directorate of Military Force Management Policy (AF/A1P) develops policies to shape and balance the Air Force's Total Force through recruiting, accessions, retirement and separations, promotions/evaluations, and other personnel elements.
- The Directorate of Force Development (AF/A1D) develops Total Force airmen through developmental, education, and career mentorship programs. AF/A1D also develops overall strategies to improve Air Force service culture through diversity and inclusion initiatives.
- The Directorate of Senior Leader Management (AF/A1L) advises on military and civilian senior personnel matters.
- The Talent Management Innovation Cell (AF/A1H) leads initiatives to develop Air Force-level policy and procedures across the talent management life cycle.
- The Directorate of Equal Opportunity (A1Q) develops equal opportunity and human relations policy.

Given the scope and complexity of the AF/A1 mission, specialized organizations are warranted. However, given this specialization, the different organizations may lack insight into one another's objectives, operations, and databases. A major goal of PPST is to represent the efforts of these specialized organizations in order to support holistic planning.

---

[15] U.S. Air Force, *Deputy Chief of Staff of the Air Force Manpower Personnel, and Services*, Headquarters Mission Directive 1-32, September 13, 2019.

The Air Force Personnel Policy Simulation Tool

The most noteworthy innovation of PPST is its ability to simulate Air Force promotion board processes so that planners can examine the policy changes discussed previously and observe the resulting outcomes. A key component of PPST is the promotion model described in Chapter 2 of this report. The model focuses exclusively on promotion planning and selection. The promotion model can be combined with other structural and statistical models contained in PPST to form a broader inventory projection capability described in Chapter 3 of this report.

Figure 1.2 gives a high-level view of the inventory projection capability, which links all PPST models together. Each simulation cycle consists of five steps that occur on an annual basis: (1) access new officers; (2) plan promotions based on zones, opportunity, and/or projected vacancies; (3) promote officers; (4) retire and separate officers; and (5) increase years of service (YOS) for officers remaining in the active-duty inventory. PPST tracks inventories of individuals with the same Air Force Specialty Code (AFSC), YOS, and demographic characteristics.

Figure 1.2. Overview of PPST

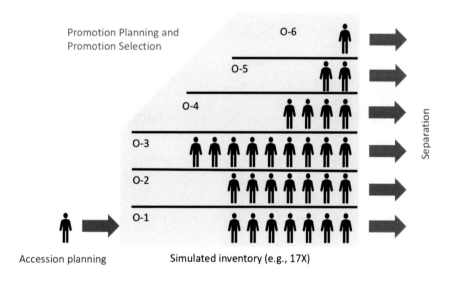

The simulation starts with the current (i.e., end of FY 2019) active-duty officer inventory and projects future officer inventories using models that represent the processes for officer accession, promotion, and retention. Accessions can be set based on planning assumptions or a mechanism that exactly replaces previous losses. Promotion planning occurs in accord with AFIs on promotion timing and promotion zones, and it takes into account grade strength considerations.[16] PPST selects officers for promotion based on a statistical model of decisions from past O-4, O-5, and O-6 promotion boards. Likewise, separations are based on a statistical model of officers'

---

[16] U.S. Air Force, *Officer Promotions and Selective Continuation*.

historical retention behaviors. In sum, PPST combines structural models of accession and promotion planning with statistical models of promotion selection and separation.

Appendix A summarizes features of PPST and compares it with other structural modeling tools for assessing the effects of personnel policy changes. A limitation of PPST (and of other structural modeling tools) is that it does not address officers' perceptions and acceptance of potential policy changes. Different research methodologies are needed to address this important dimension of policy reform, yet a tool like PPST could incorporate officer behavioral responses to policy changes through different sets of model inputs.

Organization of This Report

The remainder of this report describes PPST and presents results from simulating the effects of policy changes on career field health and demographic diversity. The chapters of the report are organized as follows:

- Chapter 2 describes the PPST promotion model and uses it to simulate the near-term effects of dividing the LAF on career field health and demographic diversity.
- Chapter 3 describes the PPST inventory projection capability.
- Chapter 4 uses the PPST inventory projection capability to simulate the long-term effects of dividing the LAF.
- Chapter 5 uses the PPST inventory projection capability to simulate the long-term effects of eliminating below-the-promotion-zone (BPZ) selections and adopting merit-based sequencing.
- Chapter 6 uses the PPST inventory projection capability to simulate the long-term effects of adopting wider promotion zones.
- Chapter 7 summarizes findings and presents directions for future research.

2. Using the PPST Promotion Model to Simulate the Near-Term Effects of Splitting the LAF

The blend of officers by career field or demographic group selected by promotion boards is influenced by two tiers of policies. The first tier of policies includes the structure of the promotion system. These policies set the timing of promotion boards, which officers are eligible to compete, and how promotion boards evaluate officers. The second tier of policies affects promotion outcomes by shaping inputs to the process. For example, grade ceiling limitations, projected strength losses, and higher-grade promotions affect promotion outcomes by limiting the total number of promotions available. Similarly, retention patterns in each career field, which are shaped by lengths of service commitments and incentive policies, affect the mix of officers who remain to compete for those promotions. These policies potentially affect various promotion and career metrics described in Table 2.1 and are referenced throughout the report.[1]

Table 2.1. Individual and Career Field Outcomes of Promotion Policies

Outcome	Description
Career field health	The number of individuals in the officer inventory by grade and career field.
Promotion opportunity	The total number of officers selected for promotion divided by the number of officers IPZ.
Selection rate	The percentage of officers in each promotion zone selected for promotion.
Phase points	The average number of years for officers selected during every one of their IPZ considerations to reach each grade.
Separation rate	The percentage of officers in a given cohort leaving the Active Component Force on an annual basis.

The interdependence between the structure of the promotion system and the policies that shape the system inputs makes it difficult to foresee the consequences of promotion policy changes. Consider the hypothetical example of decreasing the O-6 grade ceiling (i.e., the total number of individuals authorized to serve at O-6 concurrently) while holding the O-5 grade ceiling constant. This would cause O-6 promotion opportunity to decrease because the same number of officers at O-5 would be competing to fill fewer vacancies at O-6. Although the first-order effect is clear, the change would have additional effects. For example, career fields with officers who have historically fallen closer to cut lines for promotion to O-6 would be

---

[1] Promotion opportunity is calculated as the total number of officers selected for promotion in, above, and below the promotion zone divided by the total number of officers IPZ. Opportunity is used for planning purposes to set promotion quotas, and opportunity can also be used as a summary statistic to describe promotion outcomes. Selection rate is related to opportunity but is calculated as the separate percentages of officers in, above, and below the promotion zone selected for promotion.

disproportionately affected by reduced opportunity, and demographic groups overly represented in those career fields would thus be disproportionately affected as well.[2]

A second example involves the recent division of the LAF into six separate DevCats. Individuals from career fields in the same DevCat are evaluated alongside one another to be selected for a fixed number of promotions. So, the number of officers in a career field selected for promotion depends on the promotion opportunity allocated to the DevCat along with other career fields in the DevCat competing for the same share of promotions. Additionally, changes in selection rates will vary by demographic group depending on their representation in affected career fields.

PPST's promotion model represents the interplay between promotion processes and resulting outcomes, allowing planners to observe the effects of policy changes. PPST is embedded in a UI described in Appendix B. The UI allows analysts to set system parameters, such as promotion opportunity, assignment of career fields to DevCats, and weights that promotion boards give to CDEs. The promotion board model uses these inputs along with historical data to simulate promotion selections. Once simulations are completed, results and performance metrics are displayed in the UI. In this way, planners can use PPST to simulate scenarios, understand their implications, and explore policies to mitigate potential negative outcomes.

Next, we describe the promotion board model before using it to simulate the near-term effects of splitting the LAF into six DevCats.

Description of the Promotion Board Model

Before running the PPST promotion model, the user sets promotion opportunity by grade and DevCat. The user also sets the percentage of promotions allocated for below-the-zone.[3] To approximate the steady-state makeup of eligible officer cohorts, individual records spanning from 2001 to 2018 are included in the simulation. These records include CDEs for each promotion board-eligible individual along with whether they were selected for promotion. CDEs are multiplied by a set of weights and summed together to create an aggregate measure of an individual's promotability. Conceptually, this is similar to a promotion board evaluating an individual's CDEs and assigning the individual a holistic score.

The CDEs can be used to implement an entity-level model of the selection process (i.e., one in which each individual is represented separately). For example, each point in the top panel of Figure 2.1 is an officer in the 11X or 12X inventory who is eligible for promotion to O-6. The points are ordered by the individuals' promotability values. Lieutenant Colonel Smith has

---

[2] Panels are sorted by order of merit. An initial cut line is then drawn at the bottom of the score category that comes closest to filling the promotion quota without exceeding it. Individuals above the cut line are selected for promotion (AFI 36-2501). Reducing opportunity would raise the cut line, causing individuals who would have otherwise narrowly exceeded it to instead fall below it.

[3] A small percentage of promotions are given APZ as well. The tool does not contain a separate input for APZ promotions; however, these can be combined with BPZ promotions to determine the remaining number of IPZ promotions.

completed many CDEs and has high promotability, Lieutenant Colonel Brown has completed fewer CDEs and has moderate promotability, and Lieutenant Colonel Jones has completed few CDEs and has low promotability. The promotion quota is determined based on the user-specified promotion opportunity and the number of IPZ-eligible individuals. Next, a cut line is set to meet the promotion quota. Individuals to the right of the cut line are selected for promotion (Lieutenant Colonel Brown and Lieutenant Colonel Smith), while individuals to the left of the cut line are not (Lieutenant Colonel Jones).[4] We used CDEs in this way to simulate the outcomes of a single promotion board in this chapter.

Figure 2.1. Entity-Level (Top) and Cohort-Level (Bottom) Depictions of Selection Mechanism

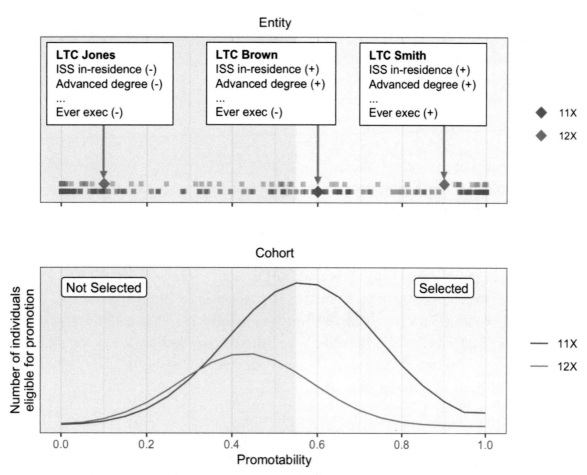

The CDEs can also be used to implement a cohort-level model of the selection process (i.e., one in which groups of individuals who share attributes like YOS and AFSC are represented together). For example, the probability distributions in the bottom panel of Figure 2.1 are estimated from the historical promotability values of individuals that make up those cohorts.

---

[4] This is a considerable but reasonable simplification of how promotion boards determine promotion quotas, assign scores to records, and establish cut lines to determine promotion outcomes (AFI 36-2501).

Again, a cut line is set to meet the promotion quota. The proportions of the 11X and 12X cohorts with promotability values to the right of the cut line are selected for promotion, and the proportions with promotability values to the left of the cut line are not. An important distinction is that individual officers (e.g., Lieutenant Colonel Brown and Lieutenant Colonel Smith) are not selected for promotion in the cohort model. Instead, proportions of officers from the 11X and 12X cohorts are selected. We used CDEs in this way to project future inventories in later chapters.

Exploring the Near-Term Effects of Splitting the LAF with the PPST Promotion Model

Historically, most Air Force officers belonged to a single DevCat. As part of the Air Force's effort to reform its talent management system, the LAF has been divided into six DevCats to allow for a wider range of developmental paths for officers while also ensuring that officers in all DevCats remain competitive for promotion. This major policy change was one of the motivating factors behind the development of PPST, and it represents an ideal use case to demonstrate how the promotion model can help planners evaluate the outcomes, both intended and otherwise, of a change to the structure of the promotion system.

Splitting the LAF into separate DevCats could affect promotion outcomes in the following way. The number of promotions potentially available to any one career field in terms of the total number of projected losses at the next grade is reduced when the LAF is split.[5] This is offset by the reduced number of officers within a given DevCat competing for those promotions. However, if the grade ceiling allocated to a DevCat differs from the total numbers of officers currently serving at each grade in career fields that make up the DevCat, those career fields may experience increased or decreased opportunity. This could be the case for career fields that have historically received more than their share of promotions relative to other career fields in the LAF.

To examine this issue, we used the PPST promotion model to simulate the near-term effects of splitting the LAF into separate DevCats. We consider two scenarios for how promotion opportunities are allocated to DevCats to illustrate the types of insights that planners can glean from the PPST promotion model.

- *Historical.* In the first scenario, we set promotion opportunity by DevCat and rank to maintain parity with historical values across career fields assigned to the same DevCat. DevCats with career fields that have historically received more than their pro rata share of promotions were given proportionately greater opportunity, and DevCats with career fields that have received fewer than their pro rata share of promotions were given lower opportunity.[6]

---

[5] The number of promotions potentially available to a career field is determined by the number of vacancies *within* its DevCat rather than *across* the complete LAF.

[6] In both scenarios, we computed the expected number of individuals selected IPZ. Based on the historical proportions of BPZ selections by AFSC and demographic group, we also computed the expected number of

- *Level.* In the second scenario, opportunity was set to the same value for all DevCats by rank.

Effects of Historical and Level Opportunity Broken Out by Developmental Category

In aggregate, the career fields that now make up the Air Operations and Special Warfare DevCat and the Combat Support DevCat have historically received a disproportionate number of promotions. This is seen in higher O-5 and O-6 opportunity for officers in those DevCats relative to officers in other DevCats (see the two "Historical" columns in Table 2.2). The proportional distribution of promotions tends to reduce O-5 opportunity in the Air Operations and Special Warfare DevCat as well as O-5 and O-6 opportunity in the Combat Support DevCat ("Historical" versus "Level" columns in Table 2.2). These reductions were offset by increases for the remaining DevCats.[7]

Table 2.2. Promotion Opportunity by Grade and Developmental Category for Historical and Level Simulations

Developmental Category	O-5 (percentage)		O-6 (percentage)	
	Historical	Level	Historical	Level
Air operations and special warfare	84	81	52	52
Space operations	66	81	43	52
Nuclear and missile operations	72	81	34	52
Information warfare	77	81	50	52
Combat support	82	81	60	52
Force modernization	79	81	43	52

Effects of Historical and Level Opportunity Broken Out by Demographic Category

The Air Force's decision to split the LAF into separate DevCats does not directly concern issues of demographic diversity. However, because the demographic makeups of career fields and the DevCats they belong to vary, a policy change that differentially affects one DevCat or career field will disproportionately affect demographic groups that are overrepresented therein.

For example, Figure 2.2 groups officers in the LAF into eight demographic groups based on gender (male or female) and race/ethnicity (black, Hispanic, white, or other). For each demographic category, the figure shows how its members are distributed among DevCats. Overall, about 50 percent of male officers and 23 percent of female officers are in the Air

---

individuals selected BPZ. From the two sets of values, we computed opportunity as the total number of selections divided by the total number of individuals who were IPZ eligible.

[7] Because the Air Operations and Special Warfare and the Combat Support DevCats accounted for more than 65 percent of officers in the O-5 and O-6 inventories, reducing selection rates in those DevCats resulted in increased selection rates for all others.

Operations and Special Warfare DevCat, whereas about 28 percent of female officers and 16 percent of male officers are in the Information Warfare DevCat. Based on these different demographic distributions, a change to the Air Operations and Special Warfare DevCat will affect more male officers than female officers; likewise, a change to the Information Warfare DevCat will affect more female officers than male officers. The distributions of white and minority officers across these DevCats follow a similar pattern, so a change to the Air Operations and Special Warfare DevCat will affect more white officers while a change to the Information Warfare DevCat will affect more minority officers.

Figure 2.2. Distribution of Developmental Categories by Race, Gender, and Ethnicity

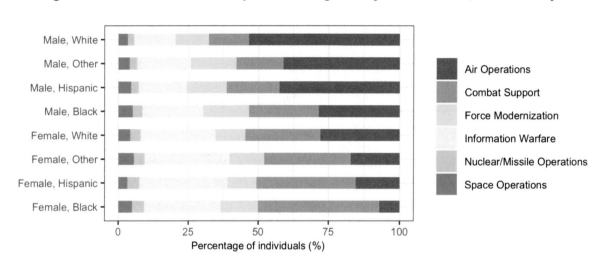

Table 2.3 contains results of the historical and level simulations grouped by gender and ethnicity. Compared with the historical scenario, the level scenario decreased O-5 opportunity for white male officers and increased O-5 opportunity for female officers, black officers, and Hispanic officers. This is because white male officers are overrepresented in career fields that make up the Air Operations and Special Warfare DevCat. The decreased number of promotions is that DevCat redistributed promotions to other DevCats and career fields with greater demographic diversity. By contrast, opportunity for promotion to O-6 remained relatively constant between the two scenarios. This is because O-6 promotion opportunity in the Air Operations and Special Warfare DevCat did not change.

Table 2.3. Promotion Opportunity by Grade and Demographic Category for Historical and Level Simulations

Gender	Ethnicity	O-5 (percentage)		O-6 (percentage)	
		Historical	Level	Historical	Level
Female	Black	75	77	46	46
Female	Hispanic	77	79	54	55

14

Gender	Ethnicity	O-5 (percentage)		O-6 (percentage)	
		Historical	Level	Historical	Level
Female	White	95	96	58	58
Male	Black	67	69	44	43
Male	Hispanic	70	71	43	43
Male	White	82	81	52	52

Summary

The Air Force's goal in splitting the LAF into six DevCats is to give officers more flexible and suitable developmental pathways within career fields while ensuring that they remain competitive for promotion. Yet the effects of splitting the LAF on promotion opportunity, promotion timing, inventory sizes, and separation rates are difficult to anticipate. To forecast these effects, we used PPST's promotion model. This simulation revealed two results.

- When promotion opportunity was equal across DevCats, career fields that historically received disproportionately more promotions (i.e., those in the Air Operations and Special Warfare DevCat) now received fewer promotions. Conversely, career fields that historically received disproportionately fewer promotions now received more promotions.
- When promotion opportunity was equal across DevCats, demographic categories (i.e., female officers, black officers, and Hispanic officers) overrepresented in career fields that have historically received disproportionately fewer promotions now received more promotions.

3. PPST Inventory Projection Capability

The PPST promotion model can help planners understand the immediate effects of promotion policies on career fields and demographic groups, but when the promotion model is used in isolation, these effects are limited to a single year's outcomes. The promotion model alone, then, cannot factor in the forces that indirectly shape future outcomes, such as the makeup of future cohorts of officers or future retention patterns. The value added of a simulation architecture that can factor in these dynamics is immense given how difficult it is to predict the ultimate result of a policy change in a system this complex. To simulate the effects of policy changes on future officer inventories, we combined the promotion model with separate models for officer accessions and separations.[1]

Combining the accession, promotion, and separation models creates an integrated inventory projection capability. As with the promotion model, this capability is embedded in a UI described in Appendix C. The UI allows analysts to set system parameters such as promotion opportunity, the percentages of promotions allocated to individuals BPZ, promotion floors, and accession policies. Once simulations are completed, longitudinal results and performance metrics are displayed in the UI.

Inventory Projection Capability

The PPST inventory projection capability combines multiple models to simulate the longitudinal effects of policy changes. These models are combined in a simulation cycle that consists of five steps that occur on an annual basis: (1) access new officers; (2) plan promotions based on zones, opportunity, and/or vacancies; (3) select and promote officers; (4) retire and separate officers; and (5) age the inventory.[2]

Accession Model

To maintain the current size of the force, the default number of annual accessions in the model is set to match the total number of annual separations. In reality, the number of accessions

---

[1] Because PPST focuses on O-5 and O-6 promotion policy changes, new accessions are somewhat less important because they do not affect results unless the time horizon is longer than the amount of time for a new officer to reach eligibility for consideration for promotion to O-5.

[2] The choice to use a one-year timestep is a simplification; many of the processes modeled (e.g., accession, separation, and effective promotion) occur continuously throughout the year.

would not perfectly match the projected or total number of separations.[3] Nonetheless the simplifying assumption that accessions equal separations provides a reasonable approximation of the average dynamics across years where the goal is to maintain the size of the force.

PPST contains two variants of this accession policy. The first assigns individuals to AFSCs to match separations. This policy maintains the size of the force *and* the size of each career field. The second policy computes the total number of separations across all career fields and assigns individuals to AFSCs in proportion to actual accession distributions in recent years. This policy maintains the size of the force but allows the size of each career field to change where recent accessions have differed from expected separations. Figure 3.1 shows accession distributions from CY 2015 to CY 2019 used in the simulation.

Figure 3.1. Percentages of Accessions by AFSC from CY 2015 to CY 2019

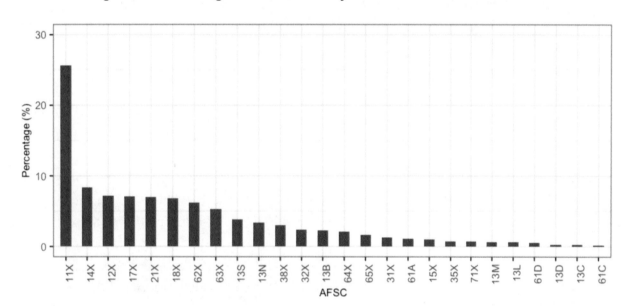

Promotion Planning and Selection Model

Simulation steps involving promotion decisions and actions were implemented in accord with AFI 36-2501 and DOPMA.[4] Key promotion parameters are summarized in Table 3.1. All individuals eligible and fully qualified for promotion to O-2 and O-3 were selected. All individuals eligible for promotion to O-4, O-5, and O-6 met promotion boards. PPST contains two mechanisms for determining the number of individuals to promote to each field grade rank.

---

[3] Air Force officer accession planning is far more complex in practice. Rated production requirements are determined based on funded requirements and projected losses. Non-rated production requirements are then determined based on the total number needed to maintain overall LAF strength minus the planned number of rated accessions. Our model does not seek to approximate this process.

[4] U.S. Air Force, *Officer Promotions and Selective Continuation.* We only simulated active-duty officers. Management of reserve officers has been governed by ROPMA.

Table 3.1. Promotion Board Timing and Selection Rules by Grade

Promotion Grade	Board Timing (Years TIG)	IPZ Rule	BPZ Rule
O-2	2Y	All fully qualified (99 percent)	–
O-3	2Y	All fully qualified (99 percent)	–
O-4	5Y	Percentage IPZ or vacancy-based	–
O-5	4Y	Percentage IPZ or vacancy-based	Percentage of authorized promotions
O-6	5Y	Percentage IPZ or vacancy-based	Percentage of authorized promotions

First, the user can supply values for promotion opportunity by grade and DevCat. In this case, the length of the promotion list for a given grade and DevCat equaled promotion opportunity multiplied by the number of individuals who were IPZ. Second, the user can choose to promote to projected vacancies. In this case, the length of the promotion list equaled the number of projected vacancies at the next highest grade and by DevCat.[5] The number of BPZ promotions was set to zero for O-2, O-3, and O-4, and the numbers of BPZ promotions were set to the lengths of the promotion lists multiplied by the corresponding BPZ percentages for O-5 and O-6.

DOPMA sets minimum TIG for officer promotions. Promotion board dates and promotion timing have historically exceeded these minimums. We based promotion timing on historical data from FY 2015 to FY 2019.[6] Table 3.1 shows board timing in terms of TIG to be considered IPZ. Individuals were considered BPZ twice before reaching the primary zone (i.e., IPZ) for promotion to O-5 and O-6, and individuals past the primary promotion zone were considered above-the-promotion-zone (APZ). In the case of O-4, O-5, and O-6, the effective date of promotion lags behind the selection date, so the minimum TIG for promotion to those grades in the simulation was delayed by one year.[7]

A critical feature of the inventory projection capability is the way that it applies the promotion model in each cycle. Certain career fields have exceeded historical LAF promotion rates while others have fallen below historical rates. This is not directly attributable to officers' career fields but rather to the CDEs they have completed, which tend to vary by career field. To capture the effects of CDEs on promotability, we analyzed officer selections by grade (O-4, O-5, and O-6) and zone (BPZ and IPZ/APZ).[8] For all board-eligible individuals, these data contain a

---

[5] Grade ceilings were based on funded authorizations plus additional allowances. The number of projected vacancies for a given grade and developmental category was based on the difference between the corresponding grade ceiling and the number of officers expected to remain in the coming year after accounting for promotions and separations.

[6] Historical promotion data provided by Air Force Personnel Center's Research, Analysis, and Data Division from their Retrieval Application Website Static Reports.

[7] Officers selected during every one of their IPZ considerations are said to have advanced in due course. Based on these values, the average phase points to reach O-2, O-3, O-4, O-5, and O-6 in due course equaled 2, 4, 10, 15, and 21 YOS.

[8] Data used to analyze O-5 selections ranged from 2009 to 2018, and data used to analyze O-6 selections, of which there are fewer, ranged from 2001 to 2018.

record of the individual's CDEs and the associated outcome (select or nonselect). We fitted logistic regression models to these data to assign promotability values ranging from zero to one to each individual based on their CDEs (Figure 2.1). Figure 3.2 shows the mean promotability values by AFSC for all individuals meeting O-5 and O-6 boards. Values vary somewhat across career fields. For example, pilots (11X) consistently have slightly above-average promotability values, whereas combat systems officers (12X) consistently have slightly below-average promotability values.

Figure 3.2. Promotability Averages by AFSC and Board

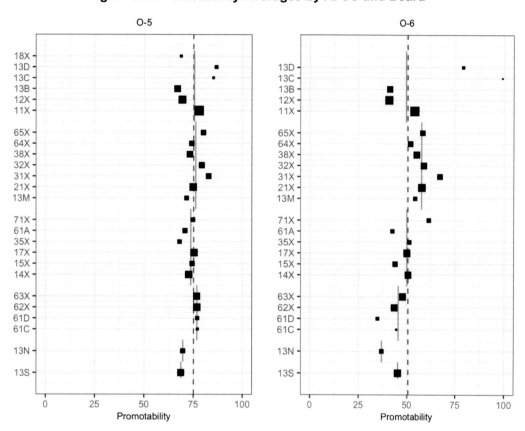

NOTE: Dashed blue lines show LAF mean promotability and red lines show mean promotability by developmental category. Squares show mean promotability by AFSC. Sizes of squares reflect relative numbers of individuals by AFSC eligible for promotion.

The values in Figure 3.2 are meant to illustrate central tendencies for promotability values by career field and grade. The promotion model uses the complete distributions of promotability values estimated from the historical data of individuals in a given cohort as described in Chapter 2 and shown in Figure 2.1.

Promotability values also vary by gender and race/ethnicity. We accounted for these factors in the promotion model as well. For some combinations of career fields and demographic groups, there were no individuals or only a small number of individuals. To derive stable estimates of promotability distributions, we used a simple rule—if the number of individuals in a given career field and demographic group was less than 30, we pooled data from all other individuals of the same gender and race/ethnicity in the same DevCat.

Controlling for career field, female officers had slightly higher promotability values than their male counterparts (Figure 3.3). This is obscured in LAF-wide values because the historical

Figure 3.3. Promotability Averages by AFSC, Demographic Category, and Board

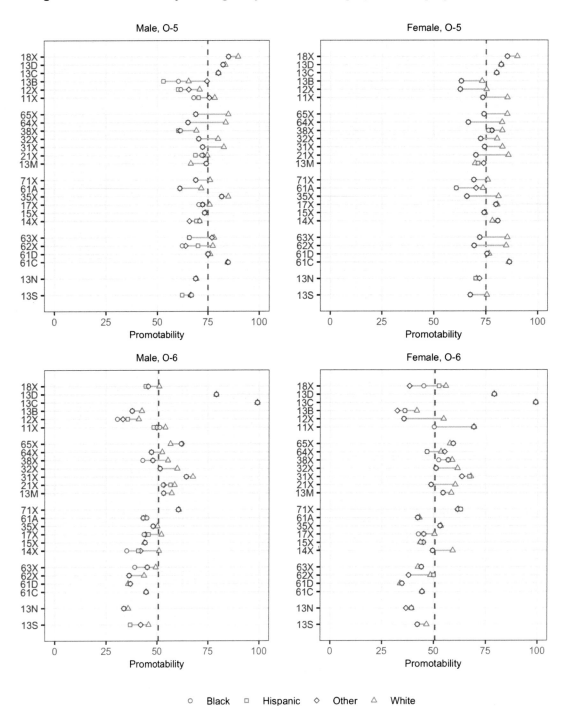

NOTE: Dashed blue lines show LAF mean promotability.

20

selection rate for the pilot career field (11X), which is extremely large and disproportionately male, is above average. Even within the 11X career field, however, mean promotability values for female officers exceeded the values for male officers. In addition to the effects of gender, the promotability values of white officers tended to exceed the promotability of black officers and Hispanic officers from the same career fields.

Separation Model

Officer retention tends to follow a predictable pattern. Initial losses are low while officers are bound by service commitments tied to commissioning programs or training (which vary by career field). After early- to mid-career losses that come at key decision points after officers satisfy initial service commitments, losses tend to be low until officers reach the retirement eligibility point of 20 YOS.

Recent annual loss rates by YOS and career field can generally approximate these patterns very well for standard inventory projections. However, to accurately capture the impact of changes in promotion policy on inventories by career field and race/ethnicity and gender, PPST requires a retention model that captures promotion status, grade, and demographic group as well. Calculating a separate loss rate for every combination of these variables, however, is not feasible.

The irregular shape of retention patterns over the course of a career, coupled with the need to account for many closely related variables, necessitates a very flexible modeling approach. We used a machine-learning algorithm to estimate a model that relates retention likelihood to YOS, grade, career field, and promotion status.[9] The algorithm systematically explores all possible combinations of the input variables to make incremental adjustments to retention predictions. Once we had a model that captured the necessary adjustments for these factors, we could then use it to predict the retention likelihood for any combination of variables that can occur in the inventory projection.

Figure 3.4 (top panel) shows estimated cumulative continuation rates (CCRs) from four AFSCs: AFSCs with high (11X and 13D), medium (15X), and low (17X) CCRs at 20 YOS. These estimates illustrate how the model captures career field differences in retention patterns. Pilots (11X) had the highest CCRs, especially through the first 12 YOS when most pilots are under training-related service commitments. Non-rated officers are eligible to separate as early as the fourth YOS, which is reflected in the CCRs for the other career fields.

Figure 3.3 (bottom panel) focuses only on the 11X career field and shows how the model captures promotion status in addition to other factors. Officers selected during every one of their

---

[9] We used a supervised machine-learning approach called a generalized boosted model implemented in the R programming language. Based on historical data, the approach learns a sequence of decision rules to predict whether an officer will separate in a given year based on their YOS, grade, career field, and promotion status. Once learned, the decision rules can be used to predict future separations. The models were fitted using Air Force personnel data from CY 2005 to CY 2018.

Figure 3.4. Model-Based Cumulative Continuation Rates by AFSC (Top Panel) and by Promotion Timing within 11X Career Field (Bottom Panel)

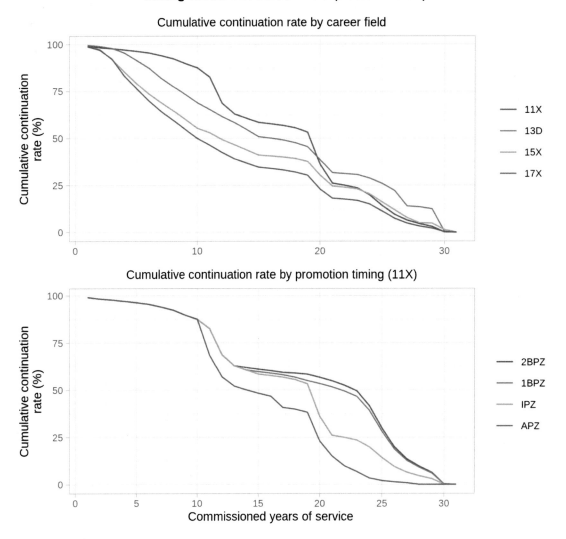

IPZ considerations are said to have advanced in due course. Individuals promoted ahead of due course (i.e., 2- or 1-BPZ) have high CCRs. This is because officers who are selected for early promotion are less likely to separate in the years after being selected and because BPZ selection signals to the individual their enhanced potential for future promotion. Conversely, individuals promoted after due course (i.e., APZ) have low CCRs. The effects of promotion timing hold across career fields.

Separation rates also vary by gender and race/ethnicity,[10] so we adapted the PPST separation model to account for these effects in addition to all previous factors (YOS, career field, and

[10] Nelson Lim, Louis T. Mariano, Amy G. Cox, David Schulker, and Lawrence M. Hanser, *Improving Demographic Diversity in the US Air Force Officer Corps*, Santa Monica, Calif.: RAND Corporation, RR-495-AF, 2014; Military Leadership Diversity Commission, *From Representation to Inclusion: Diversity Leadership for the 21st-Century Military*, Arlington, Va., 2011.

promotion status). Figure 3.5 shows model estimates for CCRs by gender and race/ethnicity while controlling for career field and promotion status. In line with previous findings, CCRs after the initial service commitment were consistently higher for male officers than for female officers. Also in line with previous findings, CCRs were higher for minority officers than for white officers.

Figure 3.5. Model-Based Cumulative Continuation Rates by Gender and Race/Ethnicity

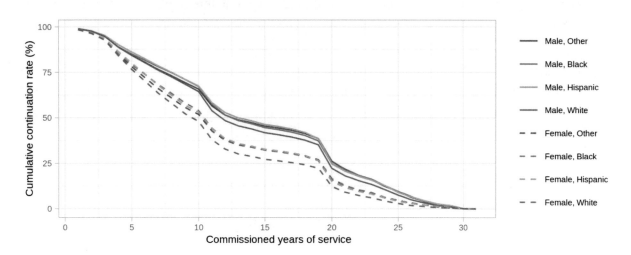

Given the complexity of the inventory projection model, we conducted extensive verification and validation to ensure that it produced accurate results (Appendix D).

Summary

The PPST inventory projection capability combines three models of accession, promotion, and separation to simulate the longitudinal effects of policy changes on officer inventories. The statistical analyses conducted to inform the promotion and separation models support three results.

- Some DevCats are made up of career fields with historically high O-6 selection rates (i.e., Combat Support), and others are made up of career fields with historically low selection rates (Force Modernization, Space Operations, and Nuclear and Missile Operations). An implication is that the grade ceilings allocated to each DevCat may cause selection rates to deviate from historical values.
- Officers selected BPZ have higher CCRs than officers selected IPZ, who in turn have higher CCRs than officers selected APZ. An implication is a policy that reduces BPZ and IPZ selection rates for a personnel category will also reduce CCRs for that category.
- Male officers have higher CCRs than female officers, and minority officers have higher CCRs than white officers. As a result, even if promotion outcomes are equated, differences in CCRs will give rise to differences among demographic groups.

4. Implications of Splitting the LAF for Future Inventories

In Chapter 2, we used the PPST promotion model to simulate the effects on a single promotion cycle of dividing the LAF into separate DevCats. These effects may be compounded over time and modulated by separation rates, accession rates, and the starting composition of the inventory. While the promotion model suggested that this change might benefit career fields and demographic groups that have historically received fewer promotions in the near term, the inventory projection capability provides quantitative predictions about the interplay between policy changes and other factors that influence inventory levels over time.

In this chapter, we illustrate the functionality of PPST by returning to the policy that divided the LAF into separate DevCats. We began these simulations with the CY 2019 officer inventory and extend over a 20-year horizon. We evaluated three scenarios.

- *Line of the Air Force (LAF).* As a baseline, we included a "do nothing" scenario that carried the historical LAF structure forward. This scenario involves a single DevCat with grade ceilings determined from funded authorizations at each grade. The numbers of promotions in this scenario were determined by projected vacancies across the LAF.
- *Split DevCats (Split).* As a first alternative, we included a scenario considered by the Air Force. This scenario involves dividing the LAF into six DevCats (see Table 2.1). The grade ceilings for each DevCat used in this scenario were determined from funded authorizations. The numbers of promotions in this scenario were determined by projected vacancies within each DevCat.
- *Restore historical opportunity (Restore).* As a second alternative, we varied promotion opportunity by DevCat to more closely mirror historical values for the career fields that make up a given DevCat. We took as a starting point the values shown in Table 4.1. To equate grade strength with the LAF simulation, we multiplied values for O-5 opportunity by 1.07, and we multiplied values for O-6 opportunity by 1.09. The numbers of promotions in this scenario were determined by the promotion opportunity specified for each DevCat.

Table 4.1. Promotion Opportunity by Grade and Developmental Category for Restore Simulation

	Grade		
Developmental Category	O-4 (percentage)	O-5 (percentage)	O-6 (percentage)
Air operations and special warfare	98	90	65
Space operations	98	90	65
Nuclear and missile operations	98	85	55
Information warfare	98	90	55
Combat support	98	85	60
Force modernization	98	85	55

For each scenario and DevCat we report four outcomes: (1) selection rate by grade and zone; (2) inventory size by grade; (3) promotion timing; and (4) separation rate. In the case of the LAF, we group career fields by DevCat when reporting results, but all career fields were combined in a single DevCat in the simulation.

Effects of Splitting the LAF Broken Out by Developmental Category

Selection Rates

Splitting the LAF caused selection rates to go down for career fields in some DevCats and to go up for career fields in others. For example, Table 4.2 shows selection rates for the largest two DevCats: Air Operations and Special Warfare and Information Warfare.[11] Selection rates for O-4 and O-5 for the Air Operations and Special Warfare DevCat dropped because the O-4 and O-5 grade ceilings place an upper bound on the combined sizes of career field inventories that make up that DevCat (see the LAF versus Split columns in Table 4.2). The O-6 IPZ selection rate rose slightly because fewer officers remained in the simulated O-5 inventory, and promotions were thus distributed among a smaller pool of promotion-eligible individuals.[12] Conversely, O-5 selection rates for the Information Warfare DevCat rose because the O-5 grade ceiling placed a lower bound on the combined sizes of career field inventories that make up that DevCat. The O-6 IPZ selection rate decreased slightly, but this was offset by the increased percentage of officers selected BPZ.

To more closely mirror historical promotion rates, we set promotion opportunity to target values contained in Table 4.1. As compared with splitting the LAF, this increased IPZ selection rates for the Air Operations and Special Warfare DevCat while reducing IPZ selection rates for most other DevCats and grades, including IPZ selection rates for O-4 and O-5 in the Information Warfare DevCat (see Restore columns in Table 4.2). Yet, as compared with the LAF simulation, BPZ selection rates in the Air Operations and Special Warfare DevCat were reduced while BPZ selection rates in the Information Warfare DevCat were raised.

Figure 4.1 shows promotion rates for all DevCats by grade and zone. For promotion to O-5, the Air Operations and Special Warfare DevCat had the highest BPZ selection rates and average IPZ selection rates in the LAF simulation (blue circles). Splitting the LAF (red squares) reduced BPZ and IPZ selection rates in the Air Operations and Special Warfare DevCat, whereas it

---

[11] The IPZ selection rates in the multiyear LAF simulation (Table 4.2) differ from those in the single year historical simulation (Table 2.2), demonstrating the danger of generalizing results from one promotion cycle to multiple future promotion cycles.

[12] The O-4 and O-5 Air Operations and Special Warfare grade ceilings used in the simulation reflect 15-percent and 19-percent decreases, respectively, from the sizes of the current inventories, whereas the O-6 grade ceiling reflects a 12-percent increase from the size of the current inventory.

Table 4.2. Selection Rates for the Air Operations and Special Warfare and the Information Warfare Developmental Categories

Grade	Zone	Air Operations and Special Warfare Selection Rate1 (percentage)			Information Warfare Selection Rate[a] (percentage)		
		LAF	Split	Restore	LAF	Split	Restore
O-6	IPZ	54	63	63	56	51	53
O-6	BPZ	4	2	2	0	2	2
O-5	IPZ	77	63	87	78	92	87
O-5	BPZ	8	4	4	1	6	4
O-4	IPZ	99	60	98	99	100	98

[a] Number selected/number considered

increased BPZ and IPZ selection rates for most other DevCats.[13] The largest gains were for the Space Operations and Combat Support DevCats, which are made up of career fields with promotion rates that have historically fallen below LAF averages. Because of their dedicated grade ceilings, selection rates increased for career fields in those DevCats.

Restoring promotion opportunity shifted IPZ selection rates to values like those from the LAF simulation (Figure 4.1, black triangles), yet BPZ selection rates remained somewhat reduced in the Air Operations and Special Warfare DevCat, and they remained raised in all others.[14] The total number of BPZ selections available equals 10 percent of the total number of selections. Under a single DevCat, a highly competitive career field (e.g., 11X) may draw a disproportionate number of BPZ selections relative to its size. When the LAF is split, those career fields receive closer to their pro rata share of IPZ *and* BPZ selections. This accounts for the decreased BPZ selection rates for the Air Operations and Special Warfare DevCat.

Inventory Sizes

Figure 4.2 shows simulated inventory sizes. Splitting the LAF decreased the O-5 and O-6 inventories in the Air Operations and Special Warfare DevCat, and it increased inventories for all other DevCats (blue circles versus red squares). These changes were driven by the dedicated grade ceilings used in the split simulation. After restoring promotion opportunity (black triangles), the sizes of the O-5 and O-6 inventories by DevCat returned to around their original values, although the Air Operations and Special Warfare DevCat remained somewhat smaller and the Information Warfare DevCat remained somewhat larger.

---

[13] If more individuals are selected BPZ, fewer promotions remain available for individuals who are IPZ. This can reduce IPZ rates even if the total number of officers promoted remains the same or increases.

[14] IPZ selection rates in the Restore simulation are less than the promotion opportunity specified in Table 4.1 because 10 percent of O-5 and O-6 promotions went to individuals BPZ.

Figure 4.1. Selection Rates by Developmental Category, Board, and Zone

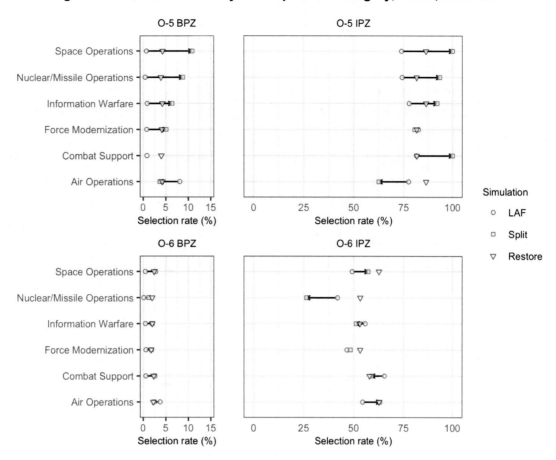

Figure 4.2. O-5 and O-6 Inventories by Developmental Category

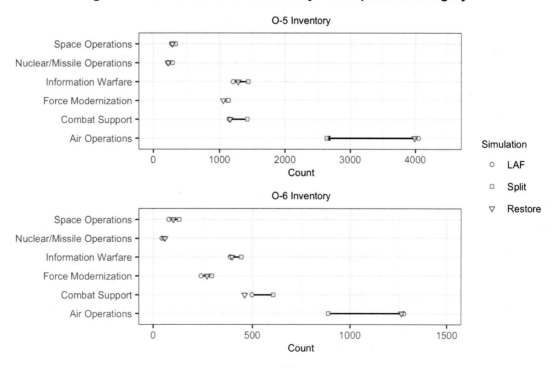

Promotion Timing

BPZ and IPZ selection rates varied by scenario. Reducing the number of BPZ selections may delay the time for officers to reach field grade ranks. Such delays may reduce the number of individuals competitive for promotion to general officer ranks (i.e., O-7); historically, nearly all individuals selected for promotion to O-7 reached O-6 with fewer than 21 YOS. As such, a policy change that reduces the number of BPZ selections in a DevCat may also reduce the number of officers in that DevCat competitive for promotion to O-7.

Figure 4.3 shows the percentage of officers by DevCat reaching O-6 ahead of due course— that is, of the officers promoted to O-6, the percentage with fewer than 21 YOS. Splitting the LAF reduced the percentage of officers who reached O-6 ahead of due course (blue circles versus red squares) in the Air Operations and Special Warfare DevCat, and it increased the percentage of officers who did so from all other DevCats. Restoring promotion opportunity reduced these changes for most DevCats (blue circles versus black triangles); however, the percentage of officers reaching O-6 ahead of due course in the Air Operations and Special Warfare DevCat still remained far lower than in the LAF simulation.

Figure 4.3. Percentage of Officers Reaching O-6 Ahead of Due Course by Developmental Category

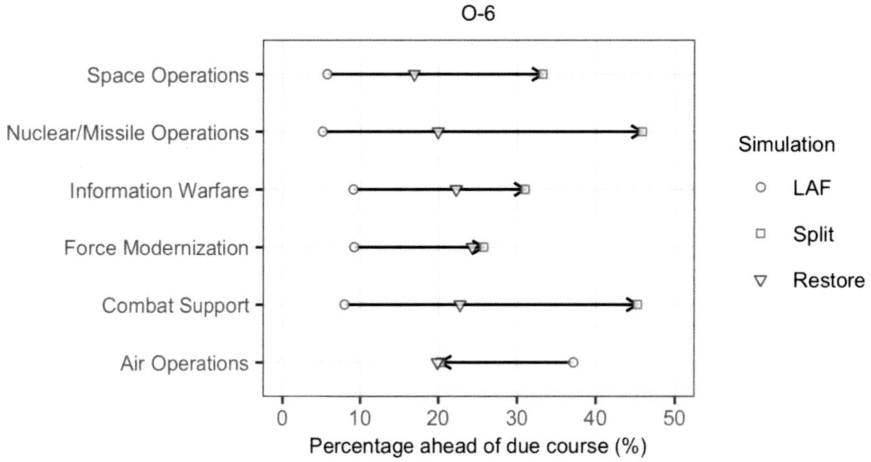

Separation Rates

Our analysis of historical retention data showed that even after controlling for AFSC and YOS, individuals selected BPZ have lower annual separation rates than those selected IPZ, who in turn have lower separation rates than those selected APZ or who were twice passed over for promotion (Figure 3.3). An implication of these retention patterns is that if fewer individuals in a DevCat are selected BPZ and IPZ, separation rates will increase.

Figure 4.4. shows CCRs for the Air Operations and Special Warfare and the Information Warfare DevCats. Splitting the LAF reduced the percentage of officers selected BPZ and IPZ in the Air Operations and Special Warfare DevCat. This indirectly reduced CCRs beginning around

Figure 4.4. Cumulative Continuation Rates for Air Operations and Information Warfare Developmental Categories

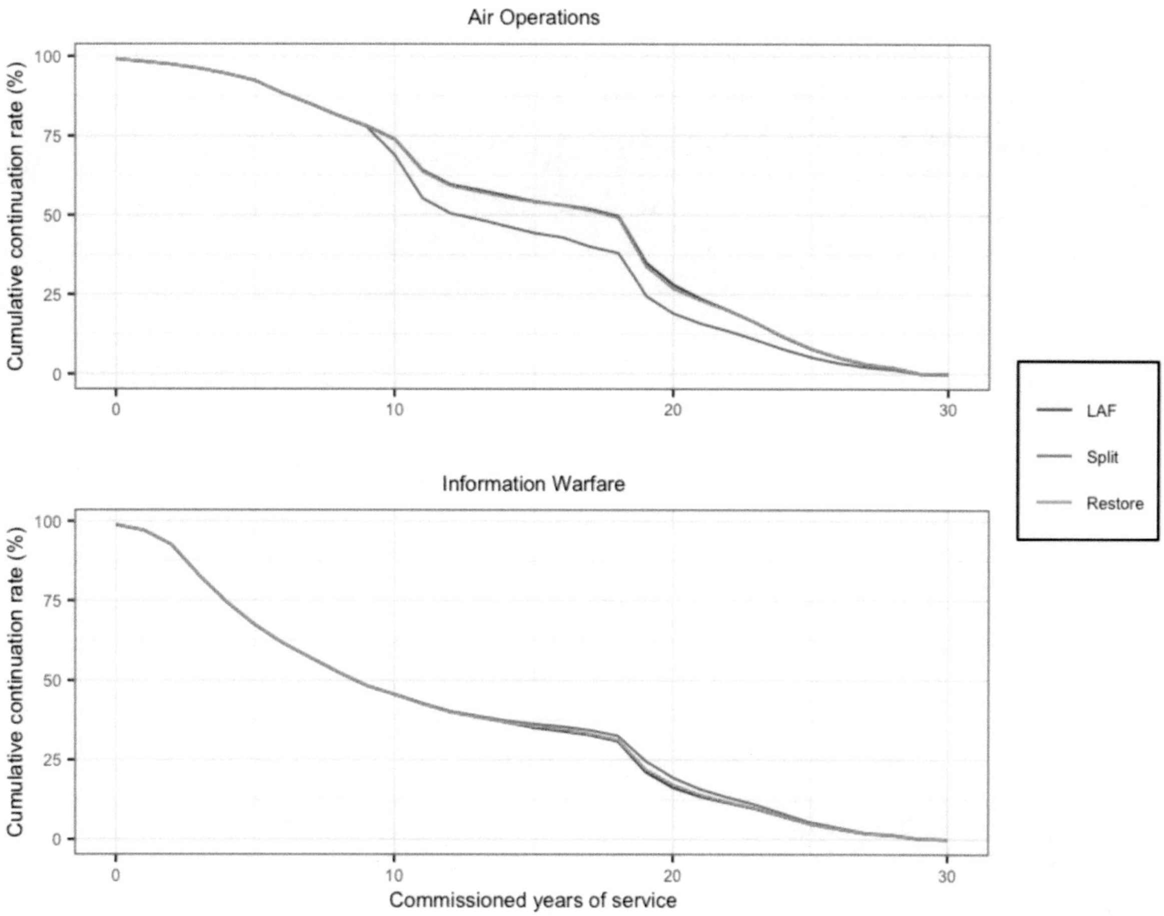

the time of O-4 promotion boards at ten YOS (top panel; blue line versus green line). Conversely, splitting the LAF increased the percentage of officers selected BPZ and IPZ in the Information Warfare DevCat, thereby increasing CCRs in that DevCat (bottom panel). Restoring promotion opportunity largely offset these changes.

Effects of Splitting the LAF Broken Out by Career Field

The effects of splitting the LAF and restoring promotion opportunity vary somewhat among career fields within the same DevCat. For example, Figure 4.5 shows simulated O-5 and O-6 inventories by AFSC. Splitting the LAF reduces the sizes of the O-5 and O-6 inventories for all AFSCs in the Air Operations and Special Warfare DevCat, yet the sizes of the reductions in absolute and relative terms are greatest for pilots (11X, blue circles versus red squares). This reflects the effect of grade ceilings on reducing the number of promotions available for pilots to compete for. Restoring opportunity increased pilot IPZ selection rates, yet BPZ rates remained depressed relative to the LAF simulation. As a result, restoring opportunity did not completely restore the 11X O-5 and O-6 inventories.

29

Figure 4.5. O-5 and O-6 Inventories by AFSC

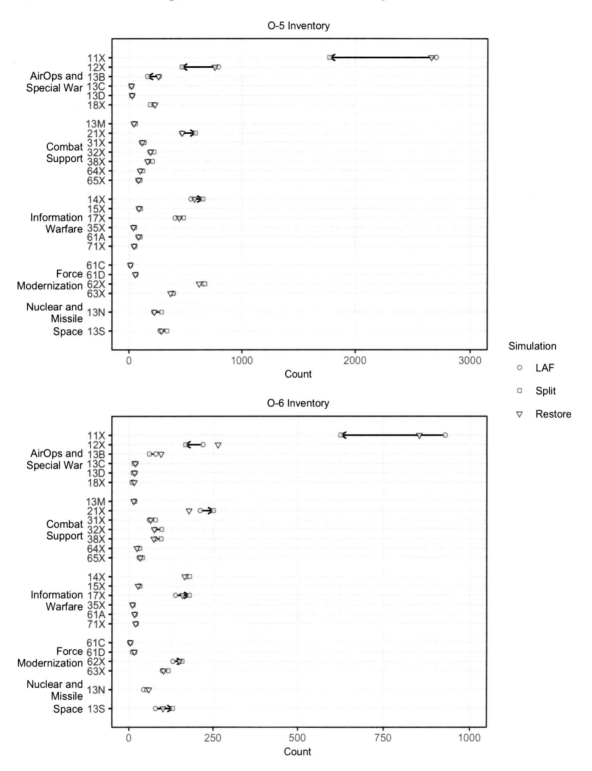

Effects of Splitting the LAF Broken Out by Gender, Race, and Ethnicity

Selection Rates

Historically, career fields that make up the Air Operations and Special Warfare category, which contain a disproportionate percentage of white male officers, have received more than their pro rata share of BPZ selections. Splitting the LAF reduced the number of selections given to career fields in the Air Operations and Special Warfare DevCat, and it redistributed them among other DevCats that contained a more balanced mix of female officers and minority officers. As a result, splitting the LAF reduced BPZ selection rates for white male officers, and it increased BPZ selection rates for officers in all other demographic groups (Figure 4.6). After restoring promotion opportunity, the effects of splitting the LAF on BPZ rates by demographic group, though smaller, were still present.

Figure 4.6. Selection Rates by Demographic Group, Board, and Zone

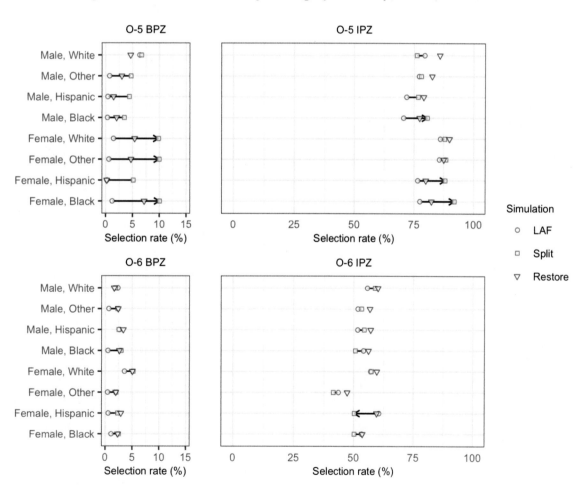

Inventory Sizes

Splitting the LAF caused the number of individuals by demographic group in the O-5 and O-6 inventories to change. These differences are shown in Figure 4.7, with values for white male officers plotted separately in the right panels because there are many times more individuals in that demographic group. Paralleling trends in selection rates, the number of white male officers in the O-5 and O-6 inventories decreased. Conversely, the number of white female officers in the O-5 inventory increased, and the numbers of all female officers and minority officers in the O-6 inventory increased. After restoring promotion opportunity, the effects of splitting the LAF on field grade inventories by demographic group, though smaller, were still present.

Figure 4.7. O-5 and O-6 Inventories by Demographic Group

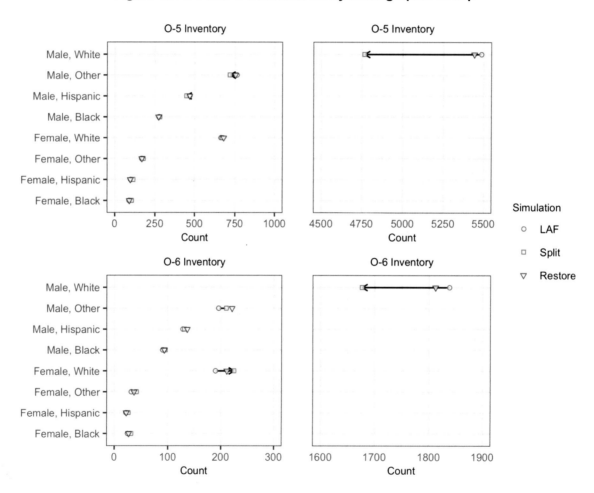

Promotion Timing

Changes in BPZ selection rates by scenario affect the time for officers to reach field grade ranks and may reduce the number of individuals competitive for promotion to general officer ranks (i.e., O-7). Splitting the LAF decreased the percentage of white male officers reaching O-6 ahead of due course, and it increased the percentages of female officers and minority officers who did so (Figure 4.8). After restoring promotion opportunity, the effects of splitting the LAF on promotion timing by demographic group, though smaller, were still present. In absolute terms, the percentage changes shown in Figure 4.8 (Restore) amount to ten more female officers and 11 more minority male officers reaching O-6 ahead of due course annually.

Figure 4.8. Percentage of Officers Reaching O-6 Ahead of Due Course by Demographic Group

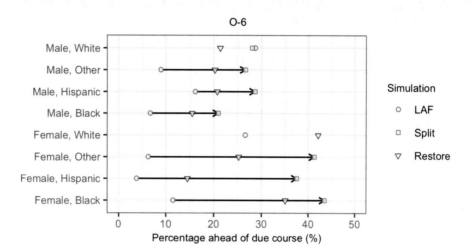

Summary

The motivation for splitting the LAF into six DevCats is to allow officers to pursue more tailored career development pathways while ensuring that they remain competitive for promotion. Yet the effects of this change in terms of promotion opportunity, promotion timing, inventory sizes, and separation rates are difficult to anticipate. To forecast these effects, we used PPST to project future officer inventories with and without the policy change. The results of our simulations with respect to career field outcomes are as follows:

- Splitting the LAF may reduce selection rates and inventory sizes, delay promotion timing, and increase separations for career fields in the Air Operations and Special Warfare DevCat.
- Splitting the LAF may increase selection rates and inventory sizes, accelerate promotions, and reduce separations for career fields in all other DevCats.
- The potentially adverse effects of splitting the LAF on career fields in the Air Operations and Special Warfare DevCat can be mitigated by setting promotion opportunity levels closer to historical values in that DevCat.
- To meet grade ceilings, increasing promotion opportunity in the Air Operations and Special Warfare DevCat must be offset by proportionally reducing opportunity elsewhere.
- Even if promotion opportunity is restored to around historical values, career fields with the highest past BPZ selection rates will receive fewer BPZ selections.

33

White male officers are overrepresented in the Air Operations and Special Warfare DevCat, and female and minority officers are overrepresented in other DevCats. Because of this, the simulated results of splitting the LAF on demographic diversity are as follows:

- Female and minority officers experienced higher BPZ and IPZ selection rates to O-5 and O-6.
- Promotion timing for female and minority officers accelerated because of their higher BPZ selection rates.
- Representation of female and minority officers at O-5 and O-6 increased because of their higher overall selection rates.
- White male officers experienced somewhat lower BPZ and IPZ selection rates and, as a result, slower promotion timing to and decreased representation at senior field grade ranks.

5. Implications of Removing Below-the-Zone Promotions and Adopting Merit-Based Sequencing

The Air Force recently announced that it plans to do away with below-the-zone promotions because of potentially adverse effects.[1] Selecting officers for early promotion affords them less time to develop before they assume additional leadership responsibilities. Further, signaling an officer's senior leadership potential too early could send a negative signal to other officers and limit the Air Force's ability to capitalize on late-emerging talent.

In place of below-the-zone promotions, the Air Force may use Section 504 of the NDAA for FY 2019, which grants promotion boards the authority to change how the order of pinning on a new rank is determined:

> In selecting the officers to be recommended for promotion, a selection board may, when authorized by the Secretary of the military department concerned, recommend officers of particular merit, from among those officers selected for promotion, to be placed higher on the promotion list established by the Secretary under section 624(a)(1) of this title.[2]

In the existing promotion system, the sequence of officers on promotion lists is determined by DOR. Officers with the earliest DOR are placed at the top of the promotion list. Merit-based sequencing, as provisioned by Section 616(h) of the Title 10, U.S. Code, could allow the Air Force to still reward high merit individuals while doing away with BPZ. Yet the effects of eliminating BPZ and implementing merit-based sequencing on promotion timing, selection rates, and separation rates are complex. To examine this issue, we extended PPST to simulate the effects of eliminating BPZ and adopting merit-based sequencing in its place.

Potential Implications of Eliminating BPZ and Adopting Merit-Based Sequencing

By statute, service secretaries establish the promotion zone for a promotion board by identifying the most junior individual eligible for in-the-zone promotion. Although not required by statute, Air Force practice is to structure the promotion zone so as to maintain year group integrity—officers commissioned in the same year are considered for promotion in the same IPZ year group. Individuals within two years of promotion zones for O-5 and O-6 are considered for below-the-zone promotion, and individuals not selected in their IPZ consideration continue to

---

[1] Stephen Losey, "Air Force to Drop Below-the-Zone Promotions for Officers," *Air Force Times*, December 10, 2019.

[2] 10 USC 616(h).

compete for above-the-zone promotion. The projected number of vacancies at the next highest grade is used to set promotion board quotas. Up to 10 percent of the quota may be allocated to BPZ selections, with the remainder going to IPZ and APZ selections.

After the selection board concludes, a promotion list is formed. The promotion list is primarily made up of officers selected IPZ (with their year-group peers) along with fewer officers selected BPZ (ahead of their year-group peers) and APZ (behind their year-group peers). Under seniority-based sequencing, individuals on the promotion list are sorted by DOR. Those with the most TIG pin on first, and those with the least TIG pin on last. BPZ selects are junior to IPZ selects, who are junior to APZ selects. Seniority-based sequencing, then, places higher-merit individuals (i.e., BPZ selects) at the bottom of promotion lists and lower-merit individuals (i.e., APZ selects) at the top of promotion lists. Nonetheless, BPZ selects are promoted ahead of their year-group peers, and APZ selects are promoted behind their year-group peers.

Doing away with BPZ and adopting merit-based sequencing could affect individuals differently. Figure 5.1 helps to illustrate how for two scenarios: a system with BPZ promotions and seniority-based sequencing (labeled *Seniority*) and a system without BPZ promotions and with merit-based sequencing (labeled *Merit*). Vertical lines display the times when promotion boards are held, and the intervals between promotion boards correspond to the promotion cycles during which individuals selected for promotion pin on the new rank. The figure displays four hypothetical officers with high, above average, below average, and low merit.

Figure 5.1. Effects of Eliminating Below-the-Promotion-Zone and Adopting Merit-Based Sequencing of Promotion Lists

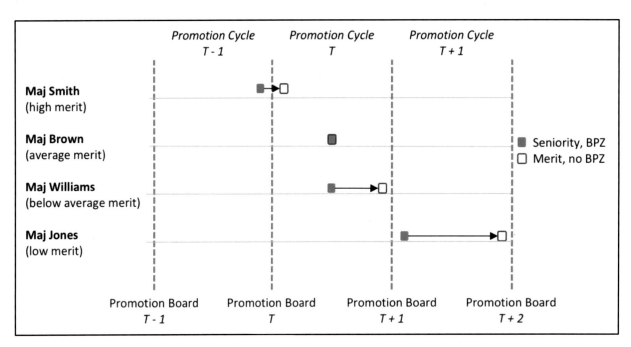

- High merit: Given seniority-based sequencing, Major Smith is selected ahead of her year-group cohort by Promotion Board *T-1* (BPZ), but she pins on at the end of Promotion Cycle *T-1* because of her low seniority relative to others selected by that board. Given merit-based sequencing, Major Smith is selected with her year-group cohort by Promotion Board *T* and she pins on at the start of Promotion Cycle *T* because of her high merit. In both scenarios, Major Smith pins on about six months earlier than others in her year-group.[3]
- Average merit: Given seniority-based sequencing, Major Brown is selected with his year-group cohort by Promotion Board *T*, and he pins on near the middle of Promotion Cycle *T* based on DOR. Given merit-based sequencing, Major Brown is again selected with his year-group cohort by Promotion Board *T*, and he pins on near the middle of Promotion Cycle *T* based on merit. In both scenarios, Major Brown pins on at about the same time as others in his year-group.
- Below average merit: Given seniority-based sequencing, Major Williams is selected with her year-group cohort by Promotion Board *T*, and she pins on near the middle of Promotion Cycle *T* based on DOR. Given merit-based sequencing, Major Williams is again selected with her year-group cohort by Promotion Board *T*, but she pins on near the end of Promotion Cycle *T* because of her below average merit. Under merit-based sequencing, Major Williams pins on about six months later than others in her year-group cohort.
- Low merit: Given seniority-based sequencing, Major Jones is selected after his year-group cohort by Promotion Board *T+1* (APZ), but he pins on near the start of Promotion Cycle *T+1* because of his high seniority relative to others selected by that board. Given merit-based sequencing, Major Jones is still selected after his year-group cohort by Promotion Board *T+1*, and he pins on near the end of Promotion Cycle *T+1* because of his low merit. Under merit-based sequencing, Major Jones pins on about a year later than the last individual in his year-group.

As the figure and examples illustrate, eliminating BPZ and adopting merit-based sequencing would produce slight delays in promotion timing for individuals of high merit, no systematic delays for individuals of average merit, and moderate to large delays for individuals of low merit.

Inventory Model Extensions

To simulate merit-based sequencing, we modified how PPST groups selected cohorts. We introduced a pair of merit thresholds used to set the upper and lower quantiles of selected officers. For example, if these thresholds are set to 10 percent, they divide the cohort of selected officers into an upper quantile (10 percent of officers with highest merit), an intermediate quantile (80 percent of officers with average merit), and a lower quantile (10 percent of officers with

---

[3] This is because Major Smith is the last to pin on during Promotion Cycle *T-1* in the first scenario and she is the first to pin on during Promotion Cycle *T* in the second scenario.

lowest merit).[4] Quantiles are applied at the level of DevCats, and so the percentages of officers in each quantile differs by career field. Splitting the selected cohort into quantiles allowed us to simulate the behavior of officers promoted earlier or later within the year based on order of merit.

We used PPST to simulate three scenarios.

1. *Baseline.* In the baseline scenario, we set O-5/O-6 BPZ allocations to 10 percent and merit thresholds to 0 percent. This emulates BPZ without merit-based sequencing, the current practice. Separation rates were based on historical values for individuals selected BPZ, IPZ, and APZ. Based on these rates, the CCRs in the top panel of Figure 5.2 show retention patterns for four subgroups of simulated individuals: those selected IPZ during each consideration (on time), those selected two years BPZ for promotion to O-5 and O-6, those selected one-year BPZ for promotion to O-5 and O-6, and those selected only after being passed IPZ (APZ).

2. *NoBPZ.* In the first alternative, we set O-5/O-6 BPZ allocations to 0 percent and merit thresholds to 0 percent. This emulates eliminating BPZ without adopting merit-based sequencing. Separation rates were based on the same historical values as before, only no officers were selected BPZ. Based on these rates, the CCRs in the middle panel of Figure 5.2 show retention patterns for two subgroups of simulated individuals: those selected IPZ during each consideration (on time) and those selected only after being passed IPZ (APZ). As compared with the baseline simulation, no individuals were promoted ahead of due course.

3. *Merit.* In the second alternative, we set O-5/O-6 BPZ allocations to 0 percent and merit thresholds to 10 percent. This emulates eliminating BPZ and adopting merit-based sequencing. As compared with BPZ with seniority-based sequencing (Figure 5.1), high merit individuals in this scenario are slightly worse off than had they been promoted one-year BPZ, and low merit individuals promoted IPZ are slightly better off than had they been promoted one-year APZ. Treating those reference groups as upper and lower bounds, we reasoned that separation rates for officers in the upper quantile would resemble individuals historically selected BPZ and that separation rates for officers in the lower quantile would resemble individuals historically selected APZ. Based on these rates, the CCRs in the bottom panel of Figure 5.2 show retention patterns for four subgroups of simulated individuals: those selected IPZ and of high merit, those selected IPZ and of average merit, those selected IPZ and of low merit, and those selected only after being passed IPZ (APZ).

In all simulations, the LAF was split into six DevCats. To facilitate comparison, grade ceilings in each simulation were set to match grade strength by DevCat in the baseline scenario.

---

[4] The merit thresholds can be set to different values. For example, setting both to 5 percent would place fewer individuals in the upper and lower quantiles, and setting them to 5 percent and 20 percent would place fewer individuals in the upper quantile and more individuals in the lower quantile.

Figure 5.2. Cumulative Continuation Rates Used in Model Simulations

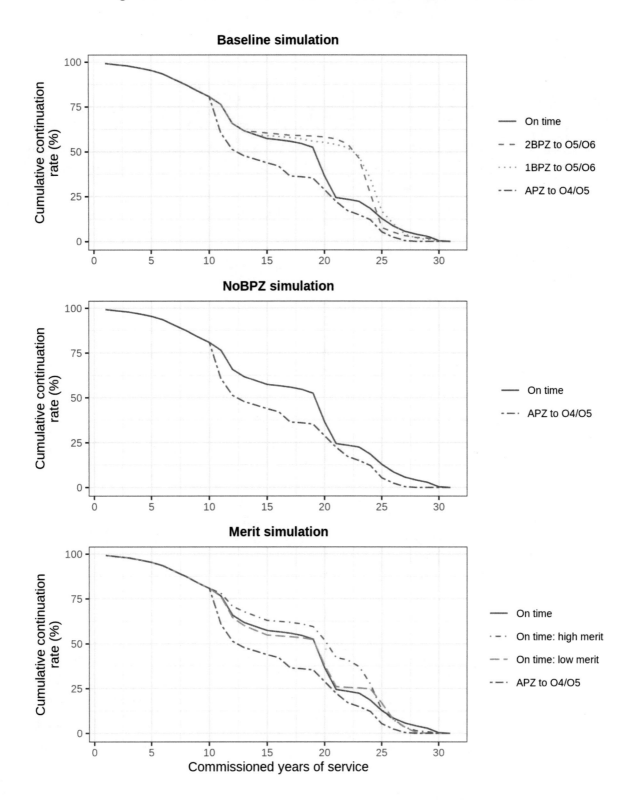

Doing away with BPZ could have at least two effects on promotion outcomes. First, individuals who would have otherwise been selected BPZ will have a higher number of YOS at selection and pin-on. By virtue of their greater age, these individuals will serve for fewer years at senior field grade ranks, causing increased separations at those ranks. Second, promotion opportunity will be artificially reduced because the IPZ cohort will include individuals who would have otherwise been selected BPZ.[5]

Doing away with BPZ without making any further changes could have at least two additional effects on retention. First, officers who would have otherwise been selected BPZ may separate before becoming IPZ eligible. Even if high-merit officers do not separate before becoming IPZ-eligible, they will not benefit from the sustained reduction in separation rates associated with a BPZ selection. Second, if the change causes more IPZ-eligible officers to be passed over for promotion, more individuals will suffer from the sustained increase in separation rates associated with an APZ selection.

Merit-based sequencing could partially counteract these adverse retention effects. As implemented in the simulation, high-merit individuals who pin on at the start of the promotion cycle are given lower sustained separation rates associated with a BPZ selection. This does not address increased YOS at pin-on, however, and so the number of years spent serving at O-5 and O-6 before separating may still decrease on average.

Aggregate-Level Effects of Zone and Sequencing Changes

Figure 5.3 (top panel) shows key metrics of annual separations, promotions, and YOS for the baseline and NoBPZ simulations. Eliminating BPZ caused a cascading sequence of effects.

- The average YOS of officers entering the O-6 inventory increased from 20.5 to 21.1 YOS. This increase reflects the elimination of BPZ selections.
- Because of their greater age, the average number of years officers spent in the O-6 inventory before separating decreased from 4.5 to 4.2 years. This caused the annual number of O-6 separations to increase from 405 to 439.
- The large number of vacancies created by O-6 separations increased the annual number of promotions to O-6. Relatedly, the large number of vacancies created by promotions to O-6 increased the annual number of promotions to O-5.
- As the number of promotions increased, fewer officers were passed over for promotion and the annual number of O-4 separations decreased.

Figure 5.3 (bottom panel) also compares the baseline scenario with one with merit-based sequencing. The results are similar to the NoBPZ simulation—the average YOS of officers entering the O-6 inventory increased, causing officers to serve for fewer years in that grade and

---

[5] Opportunity has historically been used as a metric to ensure the consistency and fairness of the promotion system. Eliminating BPZ fundamentally changes the interpretation of opportunity as previously defined and used.

Figure 5.3. Annual Separations, Promotions, and Timing in Baseline and NoBPZ Simulations

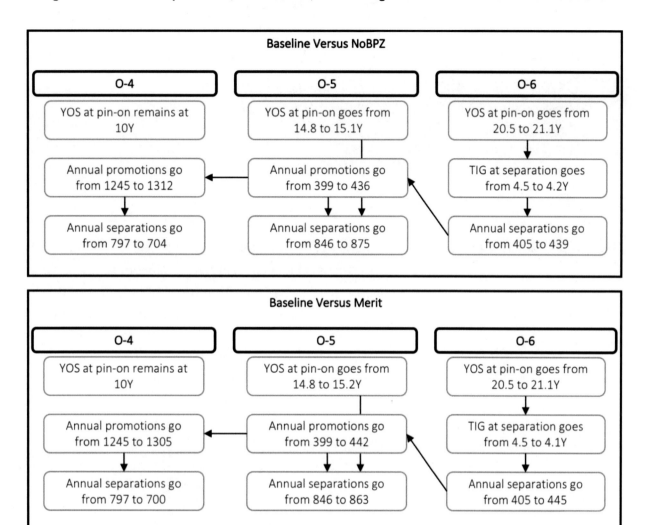

for more to separate annually. The larger number of O-6 separations created vacancies that were filled by increasing the annual number of promotions to O-5 and O-6. The annual number of O-4 and O-5 separations were slightly less than before because of the retention advantage for individuals who pinned on at the start of promotion cycles.

Table 5.1 shows promotion opportunity by grade and DevCat for the baseline simulation and each of the alternate scenarios.[6] In aggregate, O-5 and O-6 opportunity across the alternate

---

[6] Because individuals selected BPZ are removed from the IPZ-eligible cohort in the baseline simulation, opportunity in that simulation is not directly comparable with the alternate simulations. To make the scenarios comparable, we calculated the probabilities that individuals selected BPZ in the baseline simulation would have otherwise remained in the inventory until reaching the primary promotion zones. We used this adjusted value for IPZ-eligible individuals to compute opportunity in the baseline simulation.

Table 5.1. Opportunity by Grade and Developmental Category

Grade	O-5 (percentage)			O-6 (percentage)		
	Baselinea	NoBPZ	Merit	Baselinea	NoBPZ	Merit
Air operations and special warfare	83	87	87	62	69	69
Combat support	79	83	82	57	65	64
Information warfare	83	87	86	53	57	57
Force modernization	79	82	81	53	59	57
Nuclear and missile operations	79	91	90	53	55	51
Space operations	83	87	86	62	65	65
Aggregate	82	86	85	58	65	64

scenarios increased by about 4 percent and 7 percent, respectively. Changes in opportunity reflect the dual effects of increased separations on (i) increasing the number of vacancies to be filled and (ii) decreasing the number of individuals competing for promotion to fill them.

Historically, officers not selected IPZ show a spike in separation rates immediately after being passed over in the primary zone. To derive predictions for the "worst case" scenario, we conducted an additional simulation with even higher separation rates for low-merit individuals in the years when they were selected for promotion. In other words, *individuals who pin on at the end of the promotion cycle may view their placement as negatively as though they were passed for promotion.* This resulted in about seven more annual separations at O-6 and 24 more annual separations at O-4 relative to the merit-based simulation.[7]

Effects of Zone and Sequencing Changes Broken Out by AFSC

Grade strength by DevCat was fixed across each of the alternate simulations to match the baseline simulation. Grade strength by career field was allowed to vary, however. For example, if a career field received many BPZ selections in the baseline simulation, that career field would be disproportionately affected by the elimination of BPZ.

Figure 5.4 shows the annual sizes of O-6 inventories by AFSC. Inventories for AFSCs that would otherwise receive many BPZ selections (i.e., 11X) decreased when BPZ was eliminated (red squares versus black triangles). Conversely, inventories for AFSCs that would otherwise receive few BPZ selections (i.e., 12X and 13B) remained the same or increased when BPZ was eliminated. Adopting merit-based sequencing only partially restored affected inventories (red squares versus blue circles).

---

[7] The number of O-5 separations did not change because more individuals were selected for promotion to O-6 to replace losses.

Figure 5.4. Changes in O-6 Inventory Sizes by AFSC and Simulation

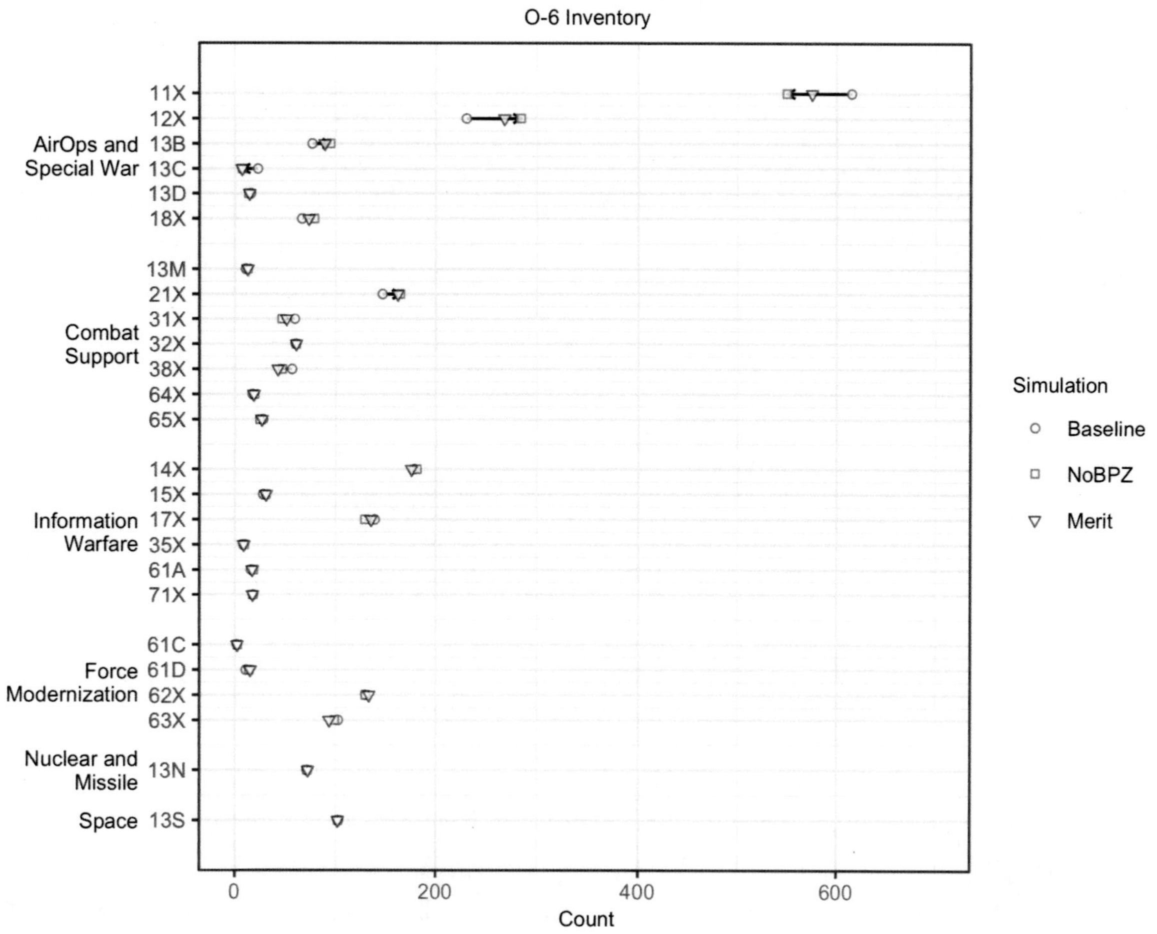

Effects of Zone and Sequencing Changes Broken Out by Gender, Race, and Ethnicity

In addition to varying by AFSC, grade strength was allowed to vary by demographic category (Figure 5.5). When BPZ was eliminated, the expected number of white female officers in the O-6 inventory decreased and the number of white male officers increased by an equal amount. Because O-6 BPZ rates for white female officers were highest among demographic groups in the baseline simulation (for review, see Figure 4.6), eliminating BPZ increased the average time for white female officers to reach O-5 and O-6, it decreased the amount of time that they served at those grades, and it reduced the sizes of the corresponding inventories. In addition, the increased vacancies allowed more white males to be selected for promotion to O-5 and O-6.

43

Figure 5.5. Changes in O-6 Inventory Sizes by Demographic Category and Simulation

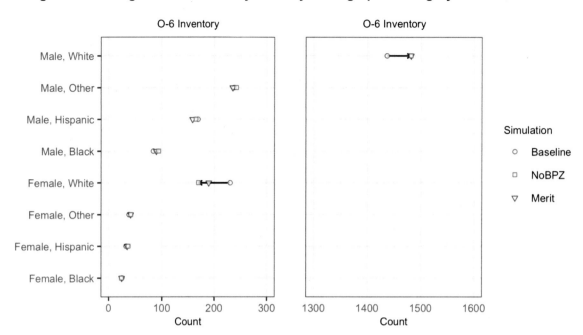

Summary

The Air Force is eliminating BPZ to increase its ability to identify and capitalize on late-emerging talent. In conjunction with this change, the Air Force is implementing merit-based sequencing to continue to reward officers of high merit. We used PPST to explore the complex effects of these structural changes on promotion timing, promotion rates, and separation rates. Our simulations showed that

- eliminating BPZ and adopting merit-based sequencing may cause a cascading series of effects involving: (1) increased average YOS for officers to reach O-5 and O-6; (2) reduced average time spent serving in those two grades; (3) increased annual separations in those two grades; and (4) increased promotion opportunity to fill vacancies resulting from separations.
- eliminating BPZ may reduce O-6 inventories for career fields that have historically received more BPZ selections (i.e., 11X) but may increase inventories in other career fields that have historically received fewer BPZ selections.
- eliminating BPZ may reduce O-6 inventories for demographic groups that would otherwise have received more BPZ selections (i.e., white female officers).
- adopting merit-based sequencing only partially offsets the effects of eliminating BPZ on O-6 inventories.

6. Implications of Widening Promotion Zones

The Air Force is considering adopting five-year promotion windows to allow for greater flexibility in career development and to allow individuals to be selected for promotion when they are developmentally ready.[1] Section 507 of the NDAA for FY 2019 grants service secretaries the authority to establish alternative promotion paths for officers in different DevCats, including altering the number of opportunities for IPZ consideration for promotion to each grade:

> In designating a competitive category of officers pursuant to section 649a of this title, the Secretary of a military department shall specify the number of opportunities for consideration for promotion to be afforded officers of the armed force concerned within the category for promotion to each grade above the grade of first lieutenant or lieutenant (junior grade), as applicable.[2]

Widening promotion windows constitutes a significant departure from long-standing officer promotion management practices. Previously, the vast majority of officers promoted to O-5 and O-6 were selected at identical points in their careers coinciding with their IPZ considerations. However, the Air Force does have precedent for distributing promotions beyond when an individual first becomes eligible. The Weighted Airmen Promotion System (WAPS) governs promotion of enlisted personnel to the ranks of E-5 through E-9.[3] Under WAPS, a failure to be selected for promotion is not viewed negatively. In fact, the WAPS formula for determining points (and the resulting order of merit) of eligible airmen results in distributions of selections that extend beyond the first consideration.

In the case of officer selection, new policy would not directly reward TIG. Rather, it would allow officers to remain competitive for selection by taking into account the CDEs they continue to complete after first being considered without penalizing them for the initial nonselection.

The effects of widening promotion zones on promotion timing, promotion rates, and separation rates are complex, and they potentially vary by career field and demographic category. To examine this issue, we extended PPST to simulate the effects of widening promotion zones.

Inventory Model Extensions

Broadening promotion zones does not require a direct change to PPST—in the inventory model, individuals passed over for promotion remain eligible for selection. However, because individuals with the highest promotability are selected from a cohort during each promotion cycle, individuals not chosen in their first consideration also tend not to be chosen in later considerations.

---

[1] Stephen Losey, "Air Force to Drop Below-the-Zone Promotions for Officers."

[2] 10 USC 616(h).

[3] U.S. Air Force, *Enlisted Airman Promotion and Demotion Program*, Air Force Instruction 36-2502, December 12, 2014.

To increase the number of officers selected after being passed over in their first consideration, we applied floors to the promotability of individuals during later considerations. These took the form of numerical boosts ranging from 0.0 to 1.0 applied to the promotability of individuals after their first consideration. This captures the idea that with increasing TIG, officers will complete additional CDEs, and so their promotability will increase. We also applied ceilings to the promotability of individuals during their first consideration. These took the form of numerical penalties ranging from 0.0 to –1.0 applied to the promotability of individuals during their first consideration. This captures the idea that with low TIG, few officers will have already completed the CDEs needed to prepare them for promotion. With these extensions in place, we used PPST to simulate three scenarios.

1. *Baseline.* In the baseline scenario, we set O-5/O-6 BPZ allocations to 0 percent. This emulates removing BPZ. No floors or ceilings were applied to promotability distributions.
2. N*th consideration floors.* In the first alternative, we applied floors ranging from 0.0 to 1.0 to the promotability of individuals during their second through fifth considerations. Floors were allowed to vary by consideration.
3. *First consideration ceiling.* In the second alternative, we applied ceilings ranging from 0.0 to –1.0 to the promotability of individuals during their first consideration. These were in addition to floors applied to the promotability of individuals during their second through fifth considerations.

In all simulations, the LAF was split into six DevCats. Promotion opportunity was anchored to the number of IPZ-eligible individuals being considered for the first time. To facilitate comparison across simulations, opportunity was set to the values by grade and DevCat as shown in Table 4.1. Separation rates were based on historical values for individuals selected IPZ.

Presently, the majority of officers promoted to O-5 and O-6 are selected during their first IPZ consideration (e.g., Figure 6.1). The Air Force has not yet identified the desired allocation

Figure 6.1. Current and Target Selection Distributions Used in Simulation

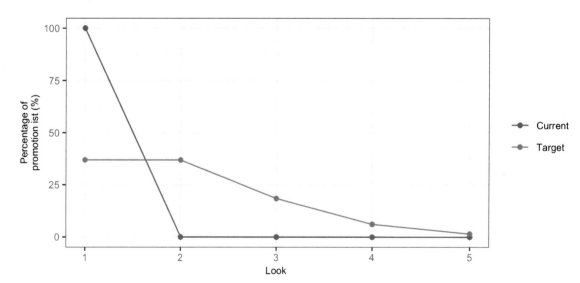

of selections across considerations, but a reasonable target to demonstrate the feasibility of widening promotion zones is to place an equal percentage of selections across the first and second considerations with a decreasing percentage of selections thereafter. We ran PPST with multiple sets of values for floors and ceilings to find values that came closest to producing the broader target distribution across five-year windows at the grades of O-5 and O-6.

Floors and Ceilings Needed to Shift Promotions

The top panel of Figure 6.2 shows the target percentages of O-5 selections by consideration (dotted black line) along with simulation results for the Air Operations and Special Warfare DevCat. Results are similar for other DevCats. In the baseline simulation, nearly all selections occur during the first consideration (red line). Applying floors after the first consideration (blue line) shifts about 25 percent of promotions from the first to the second consideration but still falls short of the target distribution. Applying an additional ceiling to the first consideration (green line) comes closest to producing the target percentages of selections by consideration.

Figure 6.2. Percentage of Promotion List and Selection Rates by Consideration

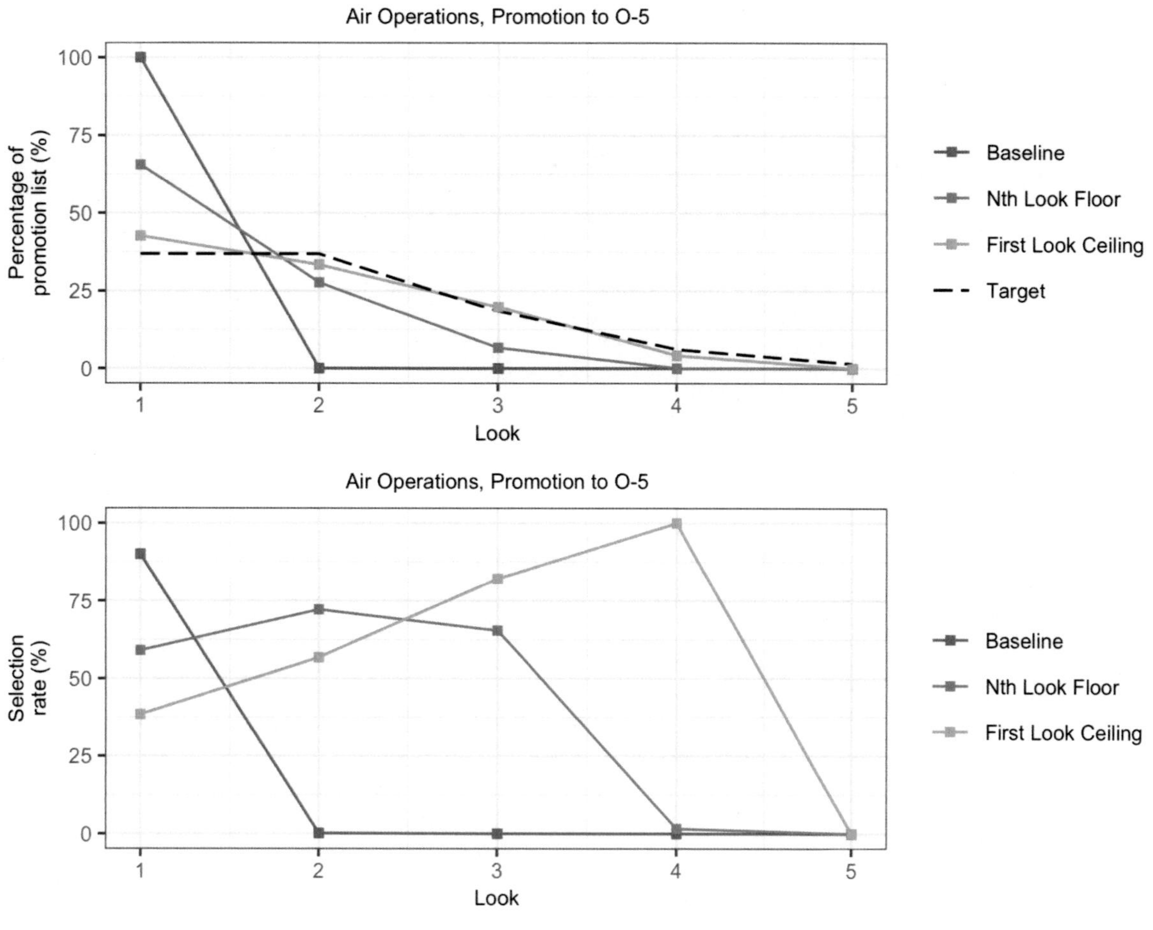

47

The bottom panel of Figure 6.2 shows corresponding selection rates by consideration. Although the percentage of selections *decreased* from the first to the fourth consideration in the simulation with ceilings and floors (green line), selection rates *increased*. This indicates that the number of individuals remaining in the inventory after each consideration decreases faster than the number that must be selected to produce the target distribution. The fact that the selection rate approaches 100 percent by the fourth look illustrates the hard upper limit on the number of individuals who could possibly be selected at or beyond that point.[4] In reality, it is unlikely that the Air Force would establish a system in which all individuals who remain beyond the third consideration are guaranteed to be selected during their fourth look.

We repeated simulations to produce the target percentages of O-6 selections by consideration (Figure 6.3). As was the case for O-5 promotions, floors and ceilings were needed to produce the

Figure 6.3. Percentage of Promotion List and Selection Rates by Consideration

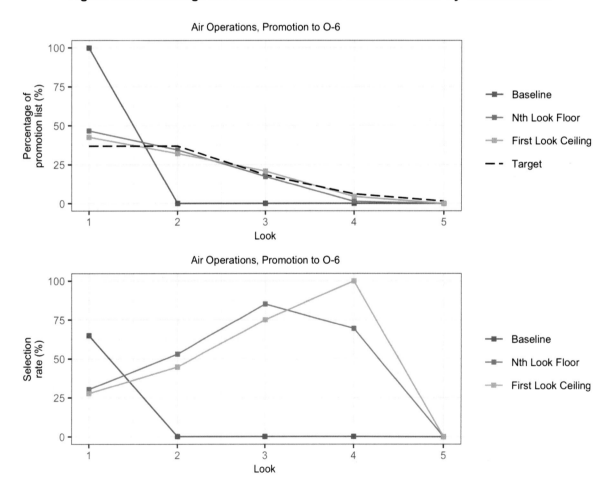

_____

[4] The number of individuals remaining in the inventory drops for each consideration due to earlier separations and selections.

target percentages of selections by consideration (green line versus dotted black line in top panel). Additionally, as the percentage of selections decreased across considerations, selection rates increased due to the decreasing number of individuals remaining in the inventory (green line in bottom panel). As was the case for O-5 promotions, selection rates approached 100 percent by the fourth look, a rate that is likely untenably high.

Table 6.1 shows values for ceilings and floors that produced the target O-5 and O-6 distributions. For context, completion and performance in Squadron Officer School (SOS) is one of the strongest past predictors of IPZ promotion to O-5. Historically, the reduced selection rates for individuals who did not complete SOS are similar in size to reductions that result when ceilings are applied in the O-5 simulation. Conversely, the increased selection rates of the top SOS graduates relative to those who did not complete SOS are similar in size to the boosts that result when floors are applied in the O-5 simulations. No other single factor considered by promotion boards, such as command experience, education, and awards, produces changes in promotability as great as those that result from the floors and ceilings used in simulation.

Table 6.1. Adjustments to Promotability Used to Produce Target Selection Distribution

| Simulation | Grade | Consideration | | | | |
		1	2	3	4	5
*N*th look floor	O-5	0.0	0.4	0.7	0.7	0.7
	O-6	0.0	0.6	0.7	0.7	0.7
First look ceiling	O-5	−0.5	−0.2	0.3	0.7	0.7
	O-6	−0.3	0.3	0.4	0.7	0.7

NOTE: Negative values denote a decrease in promotability, and positive values denote an increase in promotability.

Likewise, Senior Developmental Education (SDE) has been one of the strongest past predictors of IPZ promotion to O-6. Historically, reduced selection rates for individuals who did not complete SDE are similar in size to the reductions that result when ceilings are applied in the O-6 simulation, whereas the increased selection rates associated with completing in-residence SDE are similar to the boosts that result when floors are applied. Again, no other single factor produces changes in promotability as great as those that result from the floors and ceilings used in simulation.

Aggregate-Level Effects of Widening Promotion Zones

To determine the effects of widening promotion zones on annual separations, promotions, and phase points, we implemented floors and ceilings for promotion to O-6 in a WideZone simulation. We compared these results with the baseline simulation without floors or ceilings and while equating grade strength.[5]

Figure 6.4 shows key metrics aggregating across career fields. Widening promotion zones caused a cascading sequence of effects.

- Average YOS of officers entering the O-6 inventory increased from 20.9 to 21.6 YOS. This increase reflects the larger number of individuals selected after the first consideration.
- Because of their greater age, the average number of years officers spent in the O-6 inventory before separating decreased from 4.4 to 3.9 years. This caused the annual number of O-6 separations to increase from 422 to 461.
- The large number of vacancies caused by O-6 separations increased the annual number of promotions to O-6 from 416 to 448.
- As the number of promotions increased, fewer officers were passed over for promotion and the annual number of O-4 and O-5 separations dropped.

Figure 6.4. Annual Separations, Promotions, and Promotion Timing Across Simulated Scenarios

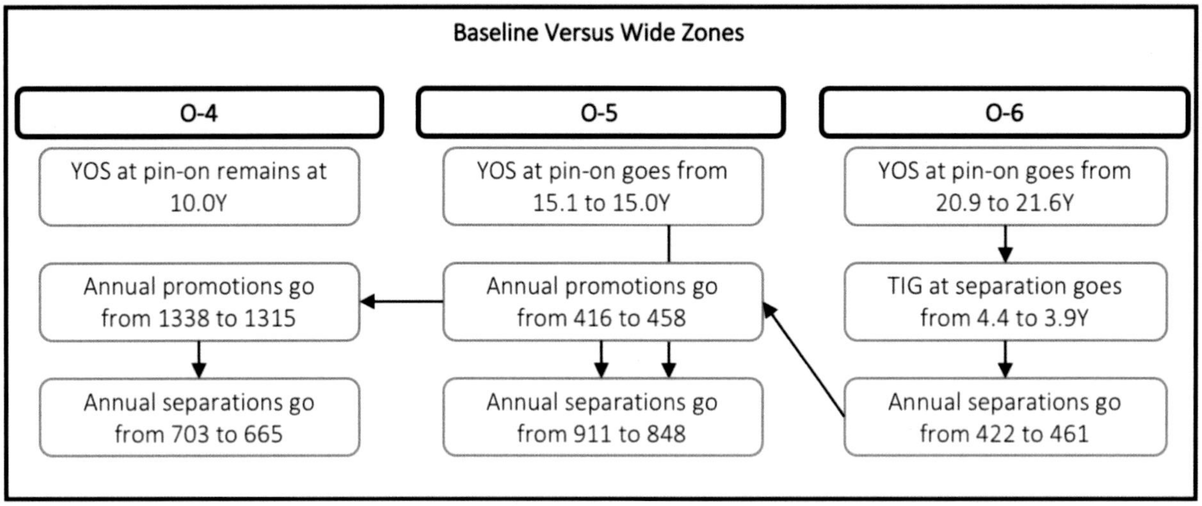

Effects of Widening Promotion Zones Broken Out by AFSC

Adopting wider zones could affect career fields in different ways. For example, the benefits of adopting wider zones may be greatest for career fields in which many individuals are not already selected during their first consideration or thereafter. In those career fields, the largest number of individuals will experience boosts in promotability after their first consideration. Alternatively, for career fields in which most individuals are selected during their first consideration, a larger number of individuals may be initially passed over for promotion.

---

[5] The floors and ceilings used in the WideZone simulation matched values for O-6 in Table 6.1.

Figure 6.5 shows the annual sizes of O-6 inventories by AFSC. Effects tended to be modest. Inventories for some AFSCs that were less competitive relative to others within the same DevCats (e.g., 21X maintainers in the Combat Support DevCat and 17X cyber operations in the Cyber/Info DevCat) increased, reflecting the greater number of individuals selected after their first consideration. Inventories for other AFSCs within the same DevCat decreased to offset those gains.

Figure 6.5. Changes in O-6 Inventory Sizes by AFSC and Simulation

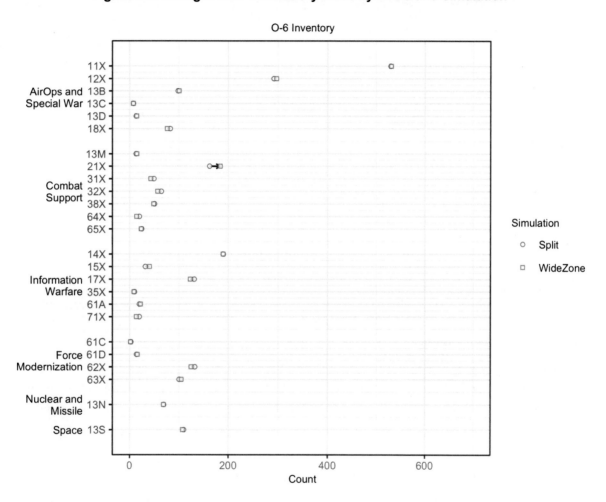

Effects of Widening Promotion Zones Broken Out by Gender, Race, and Ethnicity

As with AFSCs, adopting wider zones could affect demographic groups in different ways. However, this tended not to be the case. Figure 6.6 shows the annual sizes of O-6 inventories by demographic category. The number of white male officers in the O-6 inventory was slightly reduced, and this was offset by a modest increase in the number of black male officers and black female officers.

51

Figure 6.6. Changes in O-6 Inventory Sizes by Demographic Category and Simulation

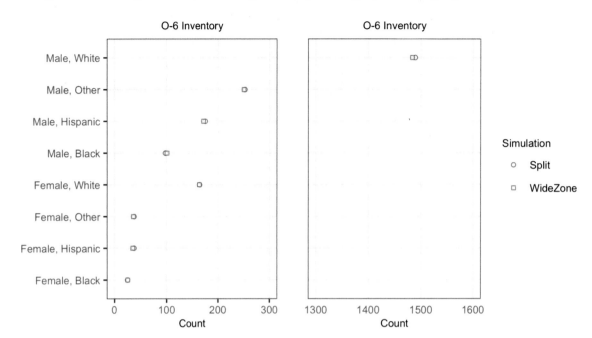

Summary

The Air Force is considering widening promotion zones to allow officers to be selected and promoted when they are developmentally ready. This is in contrast to the current system in which officers are considered for promotion when they first meet a minimum TIG requirement and in which those who are not selected during their first consideration are typically not selected during later considerations. To shift the majority of selections beyond the first consideration in simulation, it was necessary to decrease promotability during the first consideration and to increase promotability thereafter. Critically, we do not assume that promotion boards will directly adjust scores based on an officer's TIG. The adjustments in the simulation are meant to reflect the continued accumulation of experience during the years when an officer is considered for promotion. The implication is that officers must continue to complete CDEs that are visible to promotion boards and that act as strong growth signals.

We used PPST to explore the complex effects of these structural changes on promotion timing, promotion rates, and separation rates. Our simulations showed that

- for officers to become competitive for promotion after being passed during their initial consideration, they would need to complete additional CDEs visible to promotion boards and treated as significant growth signals.
- even with such a signal, officers passed over for promotion on their first consideration will likely be passed over again if the incoming cohort contains many highly qualified individuals.

- shifting an appreciable number of O-5 and O-6 selections to later considerations will increase average YOS for officers to reach those grades. Without a corresponding change to minimum TIG requirements for officers to be first considered for promotion, this will result in reduced time served and increased annual separations at the grades of O-5 and O-6.
- career fields and demographic groups with the most individuals currently passed over for promotion may experience increased selections due to the extended opportunity to develop and become competitive for promotion.

7. Discussion and Future Research

The Air Force is undertaking unparalleled reforms to its officer development and promotion management systems. As part of this reform, the Air Force has split career fields that make up the LAF into six separate DevCats. The purpose of this change is to allow officers greater flexibility to pursue tailored developmental pathways while still remaining competitive for promotion. Additionally, the Air Force is considering applications of new flexibilities allowed by the John S. McCain NDAA for Fiscal Year 2019. These flexibilities include arranging promotion lists by order of merit rather than by seniority (Section 504) and widening promotion zones to allow officers multiple IPZ considerations (Section 507). The intent behind applying these flexibilities is to allow the Air Force to identify, develop, and capitalize on talent at all points during an officer's career.

Given the complexity of the Air Force's officer personnel system, it is difficult to fully anticipate the effects of these changes. A further complication is the multitude of offices involved with officer development and promotion management, many of which have only incomplete visibility into the others' objectives, operations, and databases, yet the aspects of officer management that each office contributes to must function cohesively. These challenges are all the more significant in light of the potentially consequential effects of talent management reform on career field health and demographic diversity.

The objective of the research described in this report was to create a strategic modeling capability that both illustrates the different aspects of officer development and promotion management and simulates the effects of policy changes on career field health and demographic diversity. The resulting tool, the Air Force PPST, contains a promotion model that can be used in a stand-alone capacity or as part of a broader inventory projection capability. The simulation studies and key results generated using PPST are summarized in Table 7.1.

Table 7.1. Summary of Simulation Studies and Key Results

Chapter	Focus	Key Findings
2	Use of promotion model to simulate near-term effects of splitting the LAF on career field health and demographic diversity	• If promotion opportunity is fixed across DevCats, career fields with historically high selection rates (i.e., those in the Air Operations and Special Warfare DevCat) would experience reduced selections, and career fields with historically lower selection rates would experience increased selections. • If promotion opportunity is fixed across DevCats, demographic groups with historically high selection rates (i.e., white males) would experience reduced selections, and demographic groups with historically lower selection rates would experience increased selections.

54

Chapter	Focus	Key Findings
3	Analyses of accession, promotion, and separation data to develop statistical components of the inventory projection capability	• Some DevCats are made up of career fields with historically high O-6 selection rates (i.e., Combat Support), and others are made up of career fields with historically low selection rates (Force Modernization, Space Operations, and Nuclear and Missile Operations). • Officers selected BPZ have higher CCRs than officers selected IPZ, who in turn have higher CCRs than officers selected APZ. • Male officers have higher CCRs than female officers, and minority officers have higher CCRs than white officers.
4	Use of inventory projection capability to simulate splitting the LAF	• Splitting the LAF may reduce selection rates and the percentage of officers reaching O-6 ahead of due course in career fields with historically high selection rates (i.e., those in the Air Operations and Special Warfare DevCat) while increasing selection rates and the percentage of officers reaching O-6 ahead of due course in career fields with historically lower selection rates. • Splitting the LAF may reduce selection rates and the percentage of officers reaching O-6 ahead of due course for demographic groups with historically high selection rates (i.e., white male officers) while increasing selection rates and the percentage of officers reaching O-6 ahead of due course in demographic groups with historically lower selection rates (i.e., female officers and minority officers).
5	Use of inventory projection capability to simulate eliminating BPZ and adopting merit-based sequencing	• Eliminating BPZ and adopting merit-based sequencing may cause a cascading series of effects involving (1) increased average time for officers to reach field grade ranks; (2) reduced average time spent serving at field grade ranks; (3) increased annual separations at field grade ranks; and (4) increased promotion selections to fill resulting vacancies. • Eliminating BPZ may reduce O-6 inventories for career fields that have historically received more BPZ selections (i.e., 11X) and may increase inventories in other career fields that have historically received fewer BPZ selections. • Eliminating BPZ may reduce O-6 inventories for demographic groups that would otherwise have received more BPZ selections (i.e., white female officers). • Adopting merit-based sequencing only partially offsets the effects of eliminating BPZ on O-6 inventories.
6	Use of inventory projection capability to simulate widening promotion zones	• For officers to become competitive for promotion after first being passed, they would need to complete additional CDEs visible to promotion boards and treated as significant growth signals. • Even with such a signal, officers passed over for promotion will likely be passed over again if the incoming cohort contains many highly qualified individuals. • Shifting a significant number of O-5 and O-6 selections to later considerations would also increase average YOS for officers to reach those grades. Without a corresponding change to minimum TIG requirements for officers to first be considered, this would reduce the duration of time served and increase annual separations at field grade ranks. • Career fields and demographic groups with the most members currently passed over for promotion may experience increased selection due to the extended opportunity to develop and become competitive for promotion.

Collectively, these results speak to five general policy implications concerning officer development and promotion management.

Implication 1. The leveling effects of proposed policy changes. Splitting the LAF into DevCats with dedicated grade ceilings ensures that career fields receive closer to their pro rata share of promotions. Additionally, eliminating BPZ more closely equates promotion timing across career fields. Finally, broadening promotion zones gives officers in career fields with lower selection rates additional time to develop. On the whole, these changes will decrease selection rates in career fields that historically received disproportionately more promotions, and they will reallocate selections to career fields that historically received disproportionately fewer promotions.

Implication 2. Effects of proposed policy changes on demographic diversity due to differential representation in career fields. Career fields that have historically received disproportionately more promotions also contain a high percentage of white male officers. Therefore, policy changes that have a leveling effect across career fields will also tend to reduce selections of white male officers and increase selections of female officers and minority officers.

Implication 3. Second-order effects of proposed policy changes on promotion timing, TIG, and separation. Certain policy changes like eliminating BPZ and adopting wider promotion zones increase the average time for officers to reach O-5 and O-6. As a result, officers will serve for fewer years at those ranks, and annual separations at those ranks will increase. These effects could be mitigated by reducing minimum TIG to be considered for promotion. Yet if the goal is to allow officers more time to develop before they are promoted, an unavoidable consequence is that they will spend less of their careers at more senior grades.

Implication 4. The self-regulating nature of the officer personnel system. The officer management system has a built-in feedback loop—promotion opportunity is based on expected separations and promotions and is used to set promotion quotas. As a result, a policy change that increases separations may not reduce O-5 and O-6 inventories. Instead, it may increase the annual number of promotions to O-5 and O-6.

Implication 5. The need for strong signals to identify talent and growth. To shift a meaningful number of selections beyond the first consideration once promotion zones are widened, officers must continue to complete CDEs. The CDEs that are completed must be visible to promotion boards, and they must be treated as significant growth signals.

The simulation results show that a clear mapping from officer quality to promotion decisions is necessary for the policy changes to function as intended. Yet the possibility of significant noise in performance measurement could disrupt the intended effects, especially in the case of merit-based sequencing or wider promotion zones.

Future Research Directions

PPST provides a strategic tool for examining the effects of policy changes on career field health and demographic diversity. PPST and the research described in this report establish a basis for three continuing lines of development.

Increased Fidelity of Models Within PPST

The modular design of PPST allows for existing models to be replaced by higher fidelity models. For example, the separation models used are based on a relatively simple statistical analysis of officers' separation decisions based on career field, YOS, gender, ethnicity, and promotion history. Many other factors are associated with separation decisions and could be incorporated into a more elaborate model. Alternatively, a rational model like the Dynamic Retention Model (DRM) could be used to address compensation policy changes such as the transition to the blended retirement system in addition to these promotion policy changes.[1]

The promotion models used are based on records of CDEs that officers have completed at the time of their IPZ consideration. The fidelity of the promotion models could be increased by simulating the actual completion and timing of CDEs. This would be especially useful for understanding how the promotability of an officer increases when they are considered across multiple IPZ considerations.

Finally, officer quality maps directly to promotion decisions in PPST. The fidelity of the promotion model could be increased by taking into account how promotion boards assign scores to individuals and by allowing scores to deviate from underlying officer quality. This would be especially useful for determining whether officers can be accurately ordered by merit and whether career development can be detected when officers are considered multiple times for promotion.

Increased Functionality of PPST

As it stands, an analyst may come to PPST knowing the outcome they hope to achieve; for example, attaining a certain manning level in a career field or for a particular demographic category. The analyst then manipulates opportunity, promotion floors, and other inputs in a trial-and-error fashion to achieve that outcome. An important future direction is to include an interactive optimization routine such that the user provides the desired outcome to PPST and the application returns COAs to achieve that outcome.

User inputs in PPST are also somewhat limited. For example, certain policy interventions might be expected to increase retention. At present, an analyst may only set inputs related to

---

[1] Michael G. Mattock, James Hosek, and Beth J. Asch, *Reserve Participation and Cost Under a New Approach to Reserve Compensation*, Santa Monica, Calif.: RAND Corporation, MG-1153-OSD, 2012.

accession and promotion planning. Another important future direction is to include functionality to simulate policy changes that target other elements of personnel management.

Finally, the outputs of PPST are complex and include annual snapshots of the officer inventory by career field, rank, YOS, TIG, gender, and ethnicity. Aggregate measures like inventory sizes and promotion opportunity are informative, yet only considering results at this level of aggregation may obscure problematic outcomes that affect certain subsets of the inventory and during certain years—for example, transient decreases in manning due to a low number of company grade officers in the starting inventory for a particular career field. A final future direction is to allow analysts to set criteria that trigger warnings and that direct attention to potentially problematic outcomes contained in the simulation output.

Practical Implementation of Policy Changes

The simulation results included in this report concern the expected outcomes of policy changes *if successfully implemented*. This is separate from practical questions of how the policy changes may be implemented to be successful. Some examples include the following items:

- After splitting the LAF, will promotion boards adapt to using new criteria to evaluate officers based on their respective DevCats?
- How should evaluative criteria differ by DevCat?
- When adopting merit-based sequencing, will the complete promotion list be sorted by order of merit, or will only a subset of the promotion list be sorted?
- Are promotion board scores sufficiently accurate to enable such fine-grained sorting?
- With wider promotion zones, what combinations of experiences will increase an officer's competitiveness for promotion beyond the first consideration?
- Will officers have the opportunity to accumulate these experiences, and will promotion boards have visibility into these growth signals?
- How do officers and other key stakeholders perceive all of these potential changes?
- What steps can the AF take to increase buy-in?

PPST may indicate that a certain policy change is likely to produce the desired outcome, but PPST does not answer the question of how to practically implement the policy change.

Summary

The Air Force is undertaking major changes to its officer talent development and promotion management systems. Given the complexity of the personnel system, a strategic tool like PPST is needed to prospectively simulate outcomes of potential policy changes, identify potentially adverse effects of those policy changes, and develop mitigating COAs if called for. Our application of PPST to multiple potential policy changes suggests that they may increase parity of promotion outcomes across career fields and demographic categories. These changes will affect career field health and demographic diversity in various ways, some favorably and some unfavorably. Additional simulations and monitoring are needed as these policies are deployed.

Appendix A. Comparison of PPST with Other Approaches

Table A.1 summarizes features of PPST alongside three of RAND's other structural modeling tools for assessing the effects of personnel policies: The Military Career Model (MCM), the Dynamic Retention Model (DRM), and the Total Force Blue-Line (TFBL) Model. The MCM is a micro-simulation model that tracks simulated officers over the course of their careers, beginning from accession and extending through promotions and separation.[1] The MCM represents each individual separately, and this allows it to simulate detailed job progressions and accumulation of CDEs, whereas PPST represents groups of individuals with the same AFSC, grade, YOS, and TIG. We developed PPST for two reasons. First, PPST takes the current inventory as a starting point and simulates year-by-year effects of potential policy changes, whereas the MCM simulates the long-run (i.e., steady-state) effects of such changes. Second, PPST assigns different promotability distributions to career fields and by grade, whereas promotability of an individual in MCM can only be set when they first enter the simulation.[2]

Table A.1. Comparison of Structural Modeling Tools for Simulating Personnel Policy Changes

Simulation Element	Simulation Model			
	PPST	MCM	DRM	TFBL
Entity or cohort	Cohort	Entity	Cohort	Cohort
Simulation time step	Annual	Variable	Annual	Annual
Simulates accessions?	Yes	Yes	No	Yes
Simulates promotions?	Yes	Yes	No	No
Simulates separations?	Yes	Yes	Yes	Yes
Simulates job assignments?	No	Yes	No	No
Simulates training pipelines?	No	No	No	Yes
Career fields represented	All	All	All	Pilot
Demographic groups represented	Yes	No	No	No
Starting inventory	Provided	Simulated	Provided	Provided

---

[1] Peter Schirmer, Harry J. Thie, Margaret C. Harrell, and Michael S. Tseng, *Challenging Time in DOPMA Flexible and Contemporary Military Officer Management*, Santa Monica, Calif.: RAND Corporation, MG-451-OSD, 2006; Albert A. Robbert, Tara Terry, Alexander D. Rothenberg, Anthony Lawrence, and Neil Brian Carey, *Air Force Officer Management Flexibilities: Modeling Potential Policies*, Santa Monica, Calif.: RAND Corporation, RR-1921-AF, 2017; and Miriam Matthews, John A. Ausink, Shirley M. Ross, Matthew Walsh, Albert A. Robbert, John S. Crown, Philip Armour, Irina A. Chindea, Emily Hoch, and Sean Robson, *Championing the Agile Air Force Officer Career: Examining the Potential Use of New Career Management Flexibilities*, Santa Monica, Calif.: RAND Corporation, RR-4439-AF, forthcoming.

[2] This is done by setting an individual aptitude parameter that is static over the course of an individual's simulated career.

The DRM is a model of individuals' retention decisions over the course of their active-duty and reserve careers. The model accounts for an individual's expected military and external earnings as well as their preference for military service.[3] The DRM offers a rational model of how changes in compensation policies affect retention decisions. However, because the DRM is agnostic with respect to many other components of the officer workforce management system, it cannot be used as a stand-alone tool for modeling promotion outcomes and inventory changes.[4]

Finally, the TFBL model projects aircrew inventories in the active duty, Air Force Reserve, and Air National Guard.[5] The TFBL projections take into account the number of pilots expected to enter active duty, to separate, and to transfer into the Air Force Reserve or Air National Guard. The model uses these projections to optimize pilot assignments. Unlike PPST, which represents multiple career fields, the TFBL represents the training and production pipeline of a single career field (i.e., pilots) with high resolution. The TFBL does not contain details about officer promotion or demographic diversity, and to date it has only been applied to this one career field.

Other research has analyzed outcomes of the personnel system statistically by directly measuring the effects of factors, such as race, gender, ethnicity, source of commission, and occupation on military careers.[6] In general, these studies have shown that women leave the military at earlier career stages than men, even after controlling for a large number of nongender variables. These studies have also shown that black officers and Hispanic officers are selected for promotion at somewhat lower rates than white officers, even after controlling for a large number of nondemographic variables. Though useful for identifying factors that affect career outcomes, statistical approaches are not directly applicable to the question of *how* those outcomes would change if the structure of the workforce management system were modified. Nonetheless, statistical approaches do play an important role in two of PPST's models: one for predicting promotability and another for predicting separations.

---

[3] Mattock, Hosek, and Asch, *Reserve Participation and Cost Under a New Approach to Reserve Compensation.*

[4] The DRM could be included as a module in PPST as it has been in MCM.

[5] Tara L. Terry, James H. Bigelow, James Pita, Jerry M. Sollinger, and Paul Emslie, *User's Guide for the Total Force Blue-Line (TFBL) Model,* Santa Monica, Calif.: RAND Corporation, TL-233-AF, 2017.

[6] Beth J. Asch, Trey Miller, and Alessandro Malchiodi, *A New Look at Gender and Minority Differences in Officer Career Progression in the Military*, Santa Monica, Calif.: RAND Corporation, TR-1159-OSD, 2012; Beth J. Asch, Trey Miller, and Gabriel Weinberger, *Can We Explain Gender Differences in Officer Career Progression?* Santa Monica, Calif.: RAND Corporation, RR-1288-OSD, 2016; Susan D. Hosek, Peter Tiemeyer, M. Rebecca Kilburn, Debra A. Strong, Selika Ducksworth, and Reginald Ray, *Minority and Gender Differences in Officer Career Progression*, Santa Monica, Calif.: RAND Corporation, MR-1184-OSD, 2001; Lim, Mariano, Cox, Schulker, and Hanser, *Improving Demographic Diversity in the U.S. Air Force Officer Corps.*

Appendix B. PPST Promotion Model User Interface

PPST is implemented in the R computing language. The model is controlled from an R Shiny web application. The application is hosted on a RAND server, and so analysts in the Air Force may use the tool from an internet browser without needing to install software.

The PPST promotion model allows users to set several inputs for a single promotion board, including the following items:

- *Opportunity.* Users may manually set promotion opportunity by DevCat for promotion to O-5 and O-6. PPST allows users to provide two sets of values per grade (Options 1 and 2) to enable side-by-side comparison of different COAs.
- *Developmental categories.* Users may create new DevCats, remove existing DevCats, and assign AFSCs to different DevCats.
- *CDE weights.* Users may set the weights given to each of 12-plus CDEs historically associated with promotion outcomes. Each CDE increases an individual's probability of selection, but some CDEs are weighted more heavily than others.

PPST combines the user's inputs for promotion opportunity, the structure of the DevCats, and the CDE weights to generate simulated selection rates by career field and demographic group. Simulated selection rates can be traced back to the frequency of various CDEs by career field and demographic group along with the weights assigned to those CDEs. Model simulations take on the order of seconds to run, making it feasible to explore multiple COAs.

User Inputs

Figure B.1 shows the UI that appears when the web application is launched. The opening screen presents an overview of the application and a high-level description of the user inputs and simulation outputs.

Figure B.1. PPST Opening Page

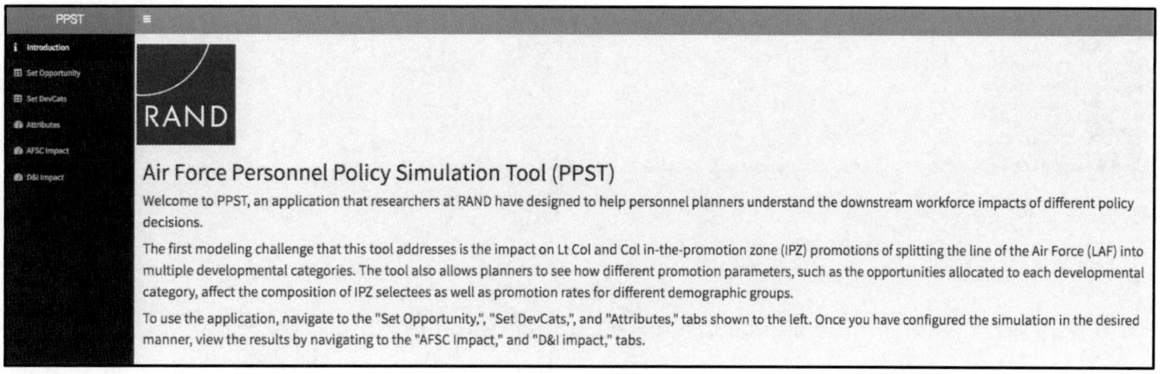

SOURCE: PPST web application.

61

The PPST promotion model allows users to observe the results of different allocations of promotion opportunities across DevCats. Figure B.2 shows the screen that appears when the user selects the "Set Opportunity" tab. The screen is divided into two subpanels corresponding to O-5 and O-6 promotion boards. For each board, the user can

- set the number of individuals eligible for promotion using the numeric input titled "Number considered."
- set the promotion quota using the numeric input titled "Number selected." When the application is first launched, the promotion quota is set to the number of individuals considered multiplied by the historical IPZ opportunity.
- set the percentage of BPZ promotions using the numeric input titled "Percentage BPZ."
- set promotion opportunity for each DevCat using the interactive table titled "O-5(O-6) Promotion Opportunity by Developmental Category." The user can supply two sets of values corresponding to Options 1 and 2.
- reset promotion opportunity to historical values using the action button titled "Reset Option 1 to historical rate" and "Reset Option 2 to historical rate."
- rescale promotion opportunity to produce the number of promotions set by the user using the action button titled "Rescale Option 1 to match grade ceiling" and "Rescale Option 2 to match grade ceiling." Promotion opportunities across DevCats are proportionately increased or decreased to meet quotas.

Figure B.2. Set Opportunity Page

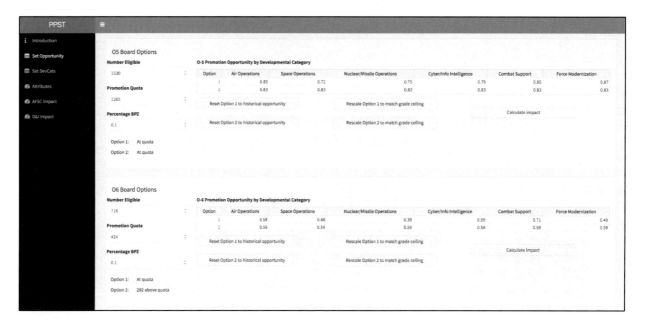

SOURCE: PPST web application.

After setting the inputs, the user runs the simulation by pressing the action button titled "Calculate Impact." The cumulative number of IPZ and BPZ selections is compared against the user-specified promotion quota to determine whether the simulation exceeds, meets, or falls below the quota. The application shows the number of promotions above or below the user-specified quotas for Options 1 and 2 below the numeric input titled "Number selected."

The DevCat structure itself is also an editable input within PPST. Figure B.3 shows the screen that appears when the user selects the "Set DevCats" tab. The table titled "Assign AFSCs to Developmental Categories" contains three-digit AFSCs in the first column and DevCats across the remaining columns. Each AFSC is assigned to one DevCat as indicated by the placement of the check mark in the row. If an AFSC is not assigned to a DevCat, the corresponding row becomes highlighted and the action button titled "Update Developmental Category Mappings" becomes disabled.

Figure B.3. Set DevCats Page

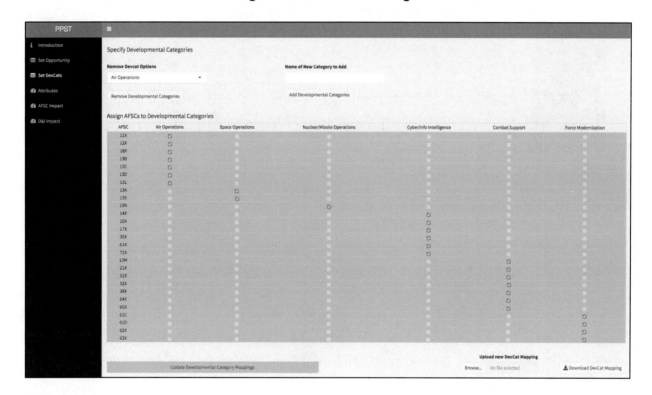

SOURCE: PPST web application.

In addition to assigning AFSCs to DevCats, the user can remove existing DevCats with the "Remove DevCat Options" pull-down menu. Likewise, the user can add new DevCats in the "Name of New Developmental Category to Add" text input field. Changes to DevCats are automatically passed to the rest of the tool.

Finally, PPST allows users to modify the weights of different CDEs in the underlying promotion model so they can observe the effect of placing greater emphasis on certain experiences or, alternatively, "masking" experiences so that board members do not consider them. Figure B.4 shows the initial screen that appears when the user selects the "Attributes" tab. In practice, promotion boards can consider CDEs differently for each DevCat and grade; the attributes tab allows the user to browse and modify CDE weights at this level. However, it is difficult to understand how to modify CDE weights without knowing how many officers would be affected. To accommodate this, the UI allows users to toggle back and forth between CDE frequencies (based on historical data) and CDE weights (based on user inputs).

Figure B.4. Comparison of Attribute Frequencies

Desirable Attribute Comparison

Officers to Display	Comparison Group
O-5	11X

Comparison of Attribute Frequency by Group and Developmental Category

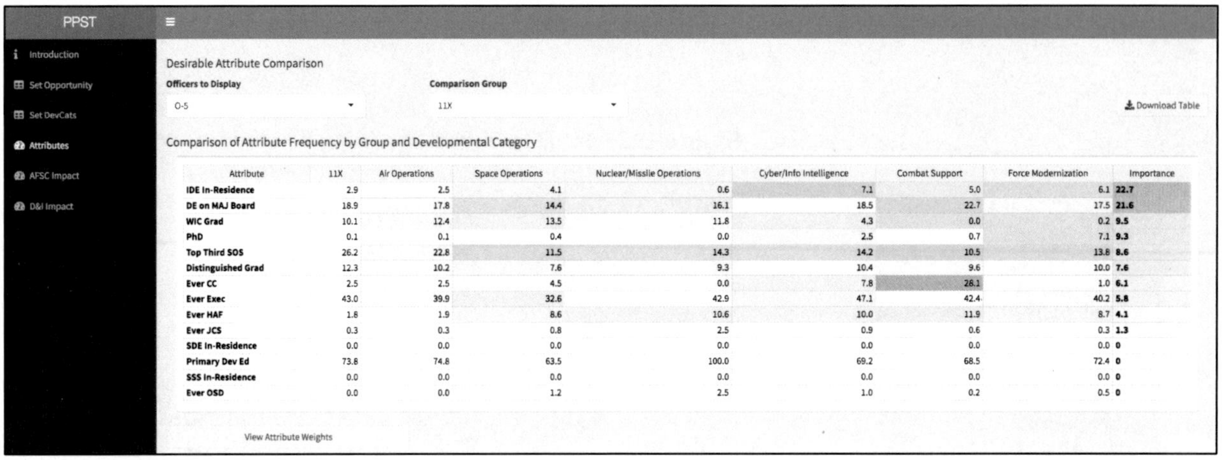

Attribute	11X	Air Operations	Space Operations	Nuclear/Missile Operations	Cyber/Info Intelligence	Combat Support	Force Modernization	Importance
IDE In-Residence	2.9	2.5	4.1	0.6	7.1	5.0	6.1	22.7
DE on MAJ Board	18.9	17.8	14.4	16.1	18.5	22.7	17.5	21.6
WIC Grad	10.1	12.4	13.5	11.8	4.3	0.0	0.2	9.5
PhD	0.1	0.1	0.4	0.0	2.5	0.7	7.1	9.3
Top Third SOS	26.2	22.8	11.5	14.3	14.2	10.5	13.8	8.6
Distinguished Grad	12.3	10.2	7.6	9.3	10.4	9.6	10.0	7.6
Ever CC	2.5	2.5	4.5	0.0	7.8	28.1	1.0	6.1
Ever Exec	43.0	39.9	32.6	42.9	47.1	42.4	40.2	5.8
Ever HAF	1.8	1.9	8.6	10.6	10.0	11.9	8.7	4.1
Ever JCS	0.3	0.3	0.8	2.5	0.9	0.6	0.3	1.3
SDE In-Residence	0.0	0.0	0.0	0.0	0.0	0.0	0.0	0
Primary Dev Ed	73.8	74.8	63.5	100.0	69.2	68.5	72.4	0
SSS In-Residence	0.0	0.0	0.0	0.0	0.0	0.0	0.0	0
Ever OSD	0.0	0.0	1.2	2.5	1.0	0.2	0.5	0

View Attribute Weights

SOURCE: PPST web application.

The table titled "Comparison of Attribute Frequencies by Group and Developmental Category" contains CDE labels in the first column along with frequencies of CDEs for a reference group in the second column (e.g., 11X) and frequencies of CDEs by DevCat across the trailing columns. The final column shows the average weights assigned to CDEs across all DevCats (normalized to sum to 100 across CDEs). The user can change the grade displayed by selecting the "Officers to Display" pull-down menu, and they can change the comparison group displayed by selecting the "Comparison Group" pull-down menu. Comparison groups that can be displayed include individual AFSCs, female officers, black officers, and Hispanic officers.

Attribute frequencies are highlighted in the table. Cells in red indicate that a lower percentage of individuals in the reference group (i.e., 11X in Figure B.4) possess the CDE than individuals in the comparison DevCats, whereas cells in green indicate that a higher percentage of individuals in the reference group possess the CDE. The intensity of the color reflects the difference between the reference group and the DevCats, weighted by the attribute's importance. Accordingly, CDEs appearing in dark green and dark red primarily drive differences in promotion outcomes between the reference group and the comparison DevCat.

64

Once the user understands the key attributes they would like to modify, they can proceed to adjust the CDE weights for each DevCat as desired. Figure B.5 shows the screen that appears when the user selects the "View Attribute Weights" action button. The table titled "Attribute Weights by Group and Developmental Category" contains names of CDEs in the first column, weights assigned to the CDEs for the reference group in the second column (i.e., 11X), and weights assigned to the CDEs by DevCat across the trailing columns. The final column shows the average weights assigned to CDEs across all DevCats (normalized to sum to 100 across CDEs). The CDEs are ordered by importance, and the row shading is proportional to each CDE's average weight.

Figure B.5. Adjusting Attribute Weights

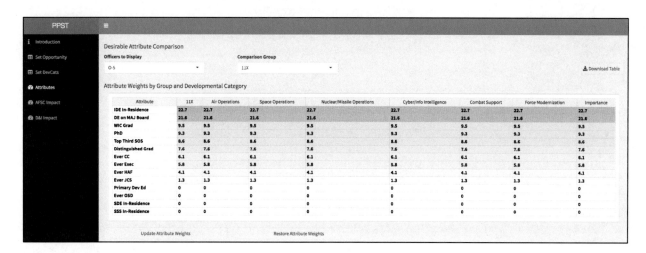

SOURCE: PPST web application.

The table is editable. To change a CDE's weight for a given DevCat, the user selects the corresponding cell and enters a new value. To commit the change, the user selects the "Update Attribute Weights" action button. The application allows the user to set weights by CDE, DevCat, and grade. To restore weights to default values, the user selects the "Restore Attribute Weights" action button. This action can be used to simulate the effects of instructing promotion boards to weight different CDEs differently and for each DevCat.

Simulation Outputs

PPST's promotion model simulates the results of a single promotion board by incorporating the user-specified opportunity, DevCats, and CDE weights into the O-5 or O-6 promotion board model. Based on user inputs, PPST generates promotion selection rates by AFSC. These outputs are displayed in the tab labeled "AFSC Impact" (Figure B.6). The first two columns show AFSCs grouped by DevCat. The next two columns show IPZ selection rates by AFSC for Options 1 and 2. These correspond to the COAs created by the user after setting different

Figure B.6. Selection Rates by AFSC and Option

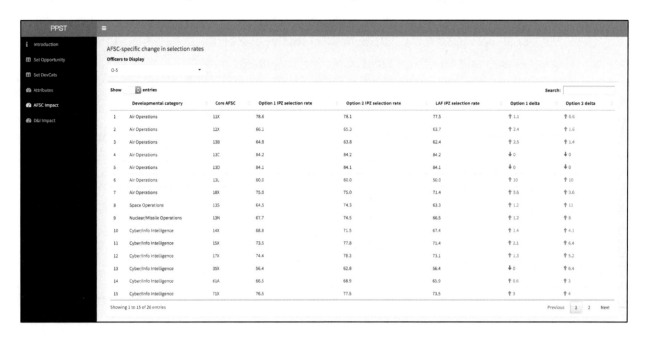

SOURCE: PPST web application.

promotion opportunities by DevCat. The next column shows the historical IPZ selection rate for the AFSC when considered as part of the LAF. The final two columns show the differences in selection rates when Options 1 and 2 are compared against historical selection rates. Green values signal increased selection rates relative to historical rates, and red values signal decreased selection rates. The user can change the grade displayed by selecting the "Officers to Display" pull-down menu.

PPST also generates selection rates by demographic group. These outputs are displayed in the tab labeled "D&I Impact," which stands for diversity and inclusion (Figure B.7). The user can change the demographic group displayed by selecting the "Demographic Group to Display" pull-down menu. Three options are available: gender, African American, and Hispanic. These options filter the portion of the officer inventory that is displayed. The user can also change the grade displayed by selecting the "Officers to Display" pull-down menu.

The bar plot at the top of the screen shows the percentage of selected individuals that come from a given demographic group. For example, for simulated Options 1 and 2, black officers made up about 2.5 percent of individuals selected for promotion to O-5 in the Air Operations DevCat (Figure B.7). The horizontal red lines show the percentage of eligible individuals that come from the same demographic group. For example, black officers also made up about 2.5 percent of individuals eligible for promotion to O-5 in the Air Operations DevCat. The key comparison is the height of the bar relative to the red line. If individuals in a particular

Figure B.7. Promotion Outcomes by Demographic Group and Developmental Category

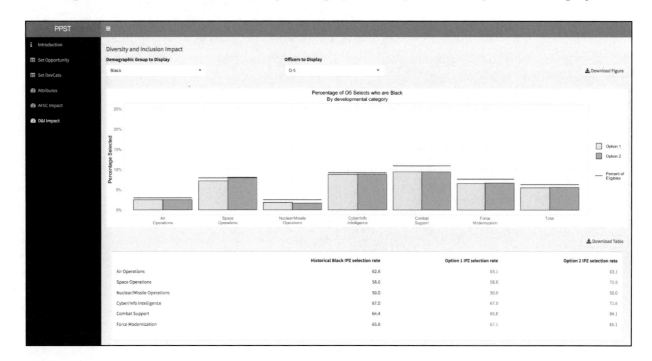

SOURCE: PPST web application.

demographic group are selected at above-average rates relative to others in the same DevCat, the height of the bar will exceed the line. Conversely, if they are selected at below-average rates, the height of the bar will fall below the line. For simulated Options 1 and 2, the representation of black officers among individuals selected for promotion to O-5 in the Air Operations Category falls below their representation among individuals eligible for promotion—a key benchmark for investigating the potential D&I impact of a series of related promotion policy changes. The rightmost bar, titled "Total," aggregates across DevCats to further provide an LAF-wide assessment of a demographic group's representation among officers eligible for promotion as well as among those selected for promotion. Once again, the representation of black officers among individuals selected for promotion to O-5 across DevCats falls below their representation among individuals eligible for promotion.

The table at the bottom of the screen contains IPZ selection rates for the active demographic group. The first column shows DevCats. The second column shows historical IPZ selection rates for individuals in the active demographic group. The final two columns show simulated IPZ selection rates for Options 1 and 2. Red values signal decreased selection rates, and green values signal increased selection rates. Absolute selection rates in the table are only indirectly related to proportional selection rates shown in the figure. For example, increasing opportunity may cause selection rates for black officers to increase. Yet if the size of the increase is greater for other demographic categories, the representativeness of, for example, black male officers among selected individuals may nonetheless decrease.

67

In summary, the PPST promotion model integrates historical board files, user inputs, and simplified selection mechanisms. Users can access the promotion model in a stand-alone application to examine how different policy alternatives (i.e., DevCat groupings, promotion opportunity, and CDE weighting) affect selection rates by career field and demographic category.

Appendix C. PPST Inventory Projection Capability User Interface

The PPST inventory projection capability can be run as a stand-alone script, or it can be controlled from an R Shiny web application. The application allows an analyst to set numerous simulation inputs.

- *Opportunity*. Users may (1) manually set promotion opportunity, (2) promote to vacancies at the next highest grade within DevCats, or (3) promote to vacancies at the next highest grade pooling across DevCats that previously made up the LAF.
- *Below-the-promotion-zone allocation*. Users may set the percentages of promotions allocated to individuals who are considered BPZ by grade and DevCat.
- *Promotion floors*. Users may set lower bounds for the numbers of individuals promoted annually by grade and AFSC.
- *Accession policy*. Users may (1) access individuals by AFSC in proportion to values from recent years (CY 2015–2019) or (2) access individuals by AFSC in proportion to projected separations.
- *Developmental categories*. By default, the simulation runs for two scenarios—one with a single DevCat and one with the LAF divided into the six DevCats.[1]

The primary results of the inventory projection capability are the numbers of individuals in the future inventory by grade and AFSC. Default results are shown for both the single DevCat and the split DevCats scenarios. Results can also be shown by simulated year. More detailed annual records of the inventory and of the numbers of individuals selected for promotion by zone, grade, and AFSC are exportable as spreadsheets.

User Inputs

Figure C.1 shows the UI that appears when the web application is launched. The opening screen provides an overview of the application and a high-level description of the inventory model and its major components.

Figure C.2 shows the screen that appears when the user selects "Run the model," at which point the user can do one of the following:

- Select the number of years to simulate.
- Choose between three promotion mechanisms: (1) vacancy-based by DevCat and grade, (2) vacancy-based by grade only, or (3) opportunity-based.

---

[1] Though not currently part of the UI, the editable DevCat table from the promotion model could be linked to this portion of PPST. We chose not to include this in the final version of the application because no additional changes to the DevCat structure are under policy consideration at this time.

Figure C.1. PPST Opening Page

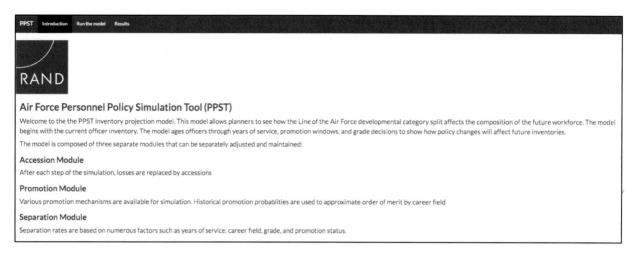

SOURCE: PPST web application.

Figure C.2. Inventory Projection Capability Setup Page

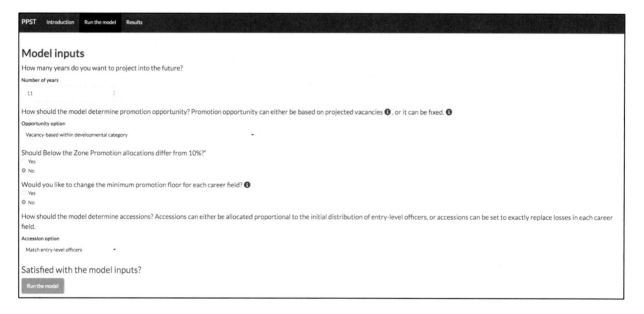

SOURCE: PPST web application.

- Set BPZ percentages by grade and DevCat.
- Set the minimum number of annual promotions by grade and AFSC.
- Choose between two accession mechanisms: (1) match recent (CY 2015–2019) accession distributions by AFSC or (2) replace annual simulated losses by AFSC.

After adjusting inputs, the user can run the model by selecting "Run the model" at the bottom of the screen. This automatically runs the model for both the single DevCat and the split DevCats scenarios.

Simulation Outputs

Once simulations are complete, the user can view the outcomes in the "Results" tab. Figure C.3 shows the screen that appears. The display shows the projected sizes of officer inventories by AFSC under two scenarios—the single DevCat (blue squares) and the split DevCats (red triangles). The arrows connecting the shapes for each AFSC show whether the projected inventories become larger or smaller after switching from the LAF to separate DevCats. AFSCs are placed along the left axis and clustered according to the six DevCats. Values for pilots are shown separately in the right panel because the 11X inventory is nearly an order of magnitude larger than all other AFSCs.

Figure C.3. Inventory Model Results Page

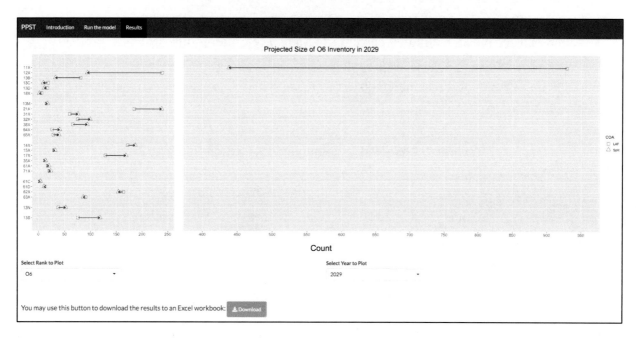

SOURCE: PPST web application.

The display in Figure C.3 contains projected O-6 inventories in 2039—the end of the 20-year simulation period. Using the pull-down menus below the plots, the user can choose to display different pay grades and simulation years. To perform additional analyses, the user can export complete simulation results as an Excel workbook.

In summary, the PPST inventory projection capability integrates historical board files, user inputs, simplified selection mechanisms, and an inventory projection model. PPST can be used to examine how different policy alternatives (i.e., DevCat groupings, promotion opportunity, and CDE weighting) affect selection rates by career field as well as how these effects are compounded over time.

Appendix D. Model Validation

To verify the model and its implementation, we performed a set of functional tests. For example, we set promotion opportunity to O-4 to zero. We expected that the number of field grade officers in the inventory would decrease to zero. This was the case. Additionally, we doubled the number of annual accessions while holding grade ceilings constant. We expected that selection rates for promotion to O-4 would be reduced because nearly twice as many individuals were competing for the same number of promotions. Again, this was the case.

To validate the model, we performed two additional tests. First, we configured the model to resemble the officer workforce management system during FY 2018. This involved simulating a single DevCat, promoting to vacancies at the next highest grade, basing grade ceilings on FY 2018 values, and allocating 10 percent of O-5 and O-6 promotions to BPZ. Table D.1 shows actual selection rates by board and zone during FY 2018 along with simulated selection rates. Simulated selection rates resembled observed rates, with the greatest discrepancy for O-5 IPZ selection rates.

Table D.1. Observed and Simulated Selection Rates by Zone

Board	Zone	LAF Selection Rate (percentage)[a]	
		Observed	Simulated
O-6	IPZ	53	53
O-6	BPZ	2	2
O-5	IPZ	72	77
O-5	BPZ	4	4
O-4	IPZ	98	96

SOURCE: PPST simulations.
[a] Number selected/number eligible.

The second test involved seeding the model with the FY 2014 inventory and performing a prospective simulation of what the FY 2019 inventory would look like. The simulated inventory could then be compared against the actual inventory to evaluate the simulation's validity over a five-year period. Each point in Figure D.1 represents a cohort, defined by AFSC and grade. If the simulated inventory perfectly matched the observed inventory, all points would fall along the main diagonal. This was roughly the case, demonstrating that over a five-year interval, the model could reasonably predict future inventories. The largest two discrepancies in absolute terms correspond to the predicted sizes of the 11X O-2 and O-3 inventories. Given that the sizes of company grade inventories are mainly driven by accession policy, this suggests some limitations in the simulation's accession model.

72

Figure D.1. Comparison of Observed and Simulated FY 2018 Inventories by Grade and AFSC

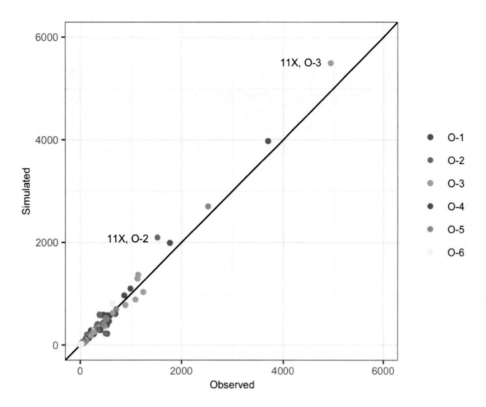

SOURCE: PPST simulations.

References

Air Force Personnel Center, *Air Force Officer Classification Directory (AFOCD): The Official Guide to the Air Force Officer Classification Codes*, October 31, 2018.

Asch, Beth J., Trey Miller, and Alessandro Malchiodi, *A New Look at Gender and Minority Differences in Officer Career Progression in the Military*, Santa Monica, Calif.: RAND Corporation, TR-1159-OSD, 2012. As of January 18, 2021:
https://www.rand.org/pubs/technical_reports/TR1159.html

Asch, Beth J., Trey Miller, and Gabriel Weinberger, *Can We Explain Gender Differences in Officer Career Progression?* Santa Monica, Calif.: RAND Corporation, RR-1288-OSD, 2016. As of January 18, 2021:
https://www.rand.org/pubs/research_reports/RR1288.html

Davis, Stephen L., et al., *Improving Air Force Squadrons—Recommendations for Vitality: Report to the Chief of Staff of the United States Air Force*, 2018.

Hosek, Susan D., Peter Tiemeyer, M. Rebecca Kilburn, Debra A. Strong, Selika Ducksworth, and Reginald Ray, *Minority and Gender Differences in Officer Career Progression*, Santa Monica, Calif.: RAND Corporation, MR-1184-OSD, 2001. As of January 18, 2021:
https://www.rand.org/pubs/monograph_reports/MR1184.html

Lim, Nelson, Louis T. Mariano, Amy G. Cox, David Schulker, and Lawrence M. Hanser, *Improving Demographic Diversity in the U.S. Air Force Officer Corps*, Santa Monica, Calif.: RAND Corporation, RR-495-AF, 2014. As of January 18, 2021:
https://www.rand.org/pubs/research_reports/RR495.html

Losey, Stephen, "Air Force to Drop Below-the-Zone Promotions for Officers," *Air Force Times*, December 10, 2019.

Losey, Stephen, "Farewell, Line of the Air Force: Massive Officer Category Broken Out into Six Groups," *Air Force Times*, October 21, 2019.

Matthews, Miriam, John A. Ausink, Shirley M. Ross, Matthew Walsh, Albert A. Robbert, John S. Crown, Philip Armour, Irina A. Chindea, Emily Hoch, and Sean Robson, *Championing the Agile Air Force Officer Career: Examining the Potential Use of New Career Management Flexibilities*, Santa Monica, Calif.: RAND Corporation, RR-4439-AF, forthcoming.

Mattock, Michael G., James Hosek, and Beth J. Asch, *Reserve Participation and Cost Under a New Approach to Reserve Compensation*, Santa Monica, Calif.: RAND Corporation, MG-1153-OSD, 2012. As of January 18, 2021:
https://www.rand.org/pubs/monographs/MG1153.html

Military Leadership Diversity Commission, *From Representation to Inclusion: Diversity Leadership for the 21st-Century Military*, Arlington, Va., 2011.

Parcell, Ann D., and Amanda Kraus, *Recommendations from the CNGR Implementation Plan: Exploring the Requirements of DOPMA and ROPMA*, Arlington, Va.: Center for Naval Analyses, CRM D0021641.A2, 2010.

Robbert, Albert A., Tara Terry, Alexander D. Rothenberg, Anthony Lawrence, and Neil Brian Carey, *Air Force Officer Management Flexibilities: Modeling Potential Policies*, Santa Monica, Calif.: RAND Corporation, RR-1921-AF, 2017. As of January 18, 2021: https://www.rand.org/pubs/research_reports/RR1921.html

Rostker, Bernard., Harry J. Thie, James L. Lacy, Jennifer H. Kawata, and Susanna W. Purnell, *The Defense Officer Personnel Management Act of 1980: A Retrospective Assessment.* Santa Monica, Calif.: R-4246-FMP, RAND Corporation, 1993. As of January 18, 2021: https://www.rand.org/pubs/reports/R4246.html

Schirmer, Peter, Harry J. Thie, Margaret C. Harrell, and Michael S. Tseng, *Challenging Time in DOPMA: Flexible and Contemporary Military Officer Management*, Santa Monica, CA: RAND Corporation, MG-451-OSD, 2006. As of January 18, 2021: https://www.rand.org/pubs/monographs/MG451.html

Secretary of Defense James Mattis, *Summary of the 2018 National Defense Strategy of the United States of America: Sharpening the American Military's Competitive Edge*, 2018.

Senate Armed Services Committee, *Modernizing the Defense Officer Personnel Management Act (DOPMA)*, SASC Staff Report, undated (copy provided during a meeting of the Manpower Roundtable, November 13, 2018).

Terry, Tara L., James H. Bigelow, James Pita, Jerry M. Sollinger, and Paul Emslie, *User's Guide for the Total Force Blue-Line (TFBL) Model,* Santa Monica, Calif.: RAND Corporation, TL-233-AF, 2017. As of January 18, 2021: https://www.rand.org/pubs/tools/TL233.html

U.S. Air Force, *Deputy Chief of Staff of the Air Force Manpower Personnel, and Services*, Headquarters Mission Directive 1-32, September 13, 2019.

U.S. Air Force, *Enlisted Airman Promotion and Demotion Program*, Air Force Instruction 36-2502, December 12, 2014.

U.S. Air Force, *Officer Promotions and Selective Continuation*, Air Force Instruction 36-2501, May 4, 2020.